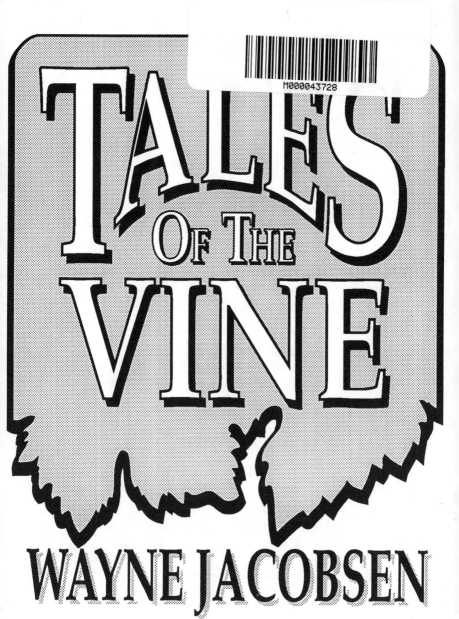

TALES
OF THE
VINE

WAYNE JACOBSEN

BODYLIFE Publishers
Visalia, CA 93277

TALES OF THE VINE
This material was originally printed as part of a work entitled,
The Vineyard (Harvest House, 1992).

Copyright © 1995 by Wayne Jacobsen
Visalia, CA 93277
209-635-8565

Jacobsen, Wayne.
Tales of the Vine/by Wayne Jacobsen
ISBN 0-9647292-0-2
Christian Life

Printed in the United States of America.

To my father and mother,

GENE AND JO JACOBSEN,

*on the occasion of their retirement
from the vineyard;
and to parents like them everywhere
who have invested their time and energy
to teach their children how to grow
in the Father's vineyard.*

CONTENTS

Acknowledgements

No one writes a book alone. There are many who contributed to the formation of this work and its publication. Let me thank a few:

- My father, Gene Jacobsen, who (after the Scriptures themselves) was my primary resource for the nature and growth of grapevines. He has spent his life teaching me the ways of God as revealed in the vineyard.
- My wife Sara, and my children Julie and Andy, who with grace and support pay a greater price than anyone else in allowing me to bring to completion the passions of my heart.
- To Bill Jensen of Harvest House for entrusting me with his idea for a book on God's vineyard.
- Eileen Mason of Mason Wheeler Communications whose editorial suggestions significantly contributed to the final product.
- To Gayle Erwin of Servant Quarters whose personal generosity and his suggestions for publishing our first work were invaluable.
- To Lance Bowen whose artistic design graces the cover and the layouts within its pages.
- To friends around the world who have encouraged my life and ministry, especially a lot of our friends who were with us at The Savior's Community when this book came together.
- To Elaine Roberts, who helped to edit the original manuscript.

Foreword

It was a bewildered group and a puzzling moment.

They had just left dinner together; a disconcerting set of hours during which their host had alternately jarred their minds and comforted their hearts.

Now He stood with them, looking across the sharp defile which suddenly fell away to the east, rising with equal suddenness to the slopes of the hill called Olives.

Scanning the scene, brilliantly lit by the full moon filling the Judean sky, His eyes sought the *exception* on this mountainside...and there it was, small and lowly among the sweeping groves of olive trees. A vine. A grapevine.

And in that setting, perhaps but an hour after having declared his new *covenant* by sharing the fruit of the vine with his dining partners, the Son of Man now drew them to study the vine as the essence of the new *relationship* He was announcing.

Three days before, on this same terrain, He had cursed a fig tree. The morbid message of its shriveled frame was mute testimony to this Prophet's word of power: The old order is dead. The tree that symbolized a disappearing era of God's dealings and reflected the fruitless response to God's call may likely have been silhouetted against the moonlit backdrop somewhere nearby.

Winding their way down the Kidron's banks, then up toward the garden they frequented as a rest stop, Jesus pauses beside the vine which is just beginning to put forth its spring-time shoots, and there He declares the nature of the new order: "I am the vine. You are the branches" (John 15:1).

While no one can confirm my description of the setting in which our Lord gave us the words which John's Gospel unfolds so poetically, powerfully and preciously, none of us can escape the importance and implications of their content. Since my training days for ministry these words have kept my soul very low at His feet: *"Without me you can do nothing"* (John 15:5). And since my first pastorate thee words have encouraged my heart: *"Your fruit shall remain"* (John 15:16c).

On the night before He died, Jesus not only unveiled the rite by which the New Covenant would be celebrated in continuum, He also engraved a symbol on the minds of His disciples. The vine was to be the key to their understanding how both relationship *with* God and fruitfulness *for* Him would be realized. Just as surely as the Lamb shortly satisfied all the legal demands of the Old Covenant, the Lord of the New Covenant testified to the pathway of life just about to open through the expiating redemption of His cross and the explosive release of His resurrection.

**The vine was to be the key
to their understanding how both
relationship *with* God and fruitfulness
for Him would be realized.**

From the day I sat as a teenager in a California church building and heard the Savior whisper to me, "You have not chosen Me, but I have chosen you" (John 15:16a), I have been increasingly aware of my dependency upon living out the vine-branch relationship with my Savior/Commissioner. And that's why I welcome this book.

In a stirring, often heart-touching, probing and personal way, Wayne Jacobsen gives us a fresh look at time-less truth. His experiences as a boy growing up on a grape ranch provides resources full of insight, which I think you'll find as enriching as you'll find them well-written. No one can write such words without having experienced more than a ranch. Here are the words of a man who has tasted the reality of a growing, impas-sioned deepening life with Jesus Himself. And that's why I want to read—and listen with my heart. Because Wayne is talking about *how* Jesus spoke of our deepen-ing relationship with Him. And I think that you, as I have, will hear Jesus' voice drawing you closer to him through Wayne's words. May it be so for us both.

Jack W. Hayford, D. Litt.
Senior Pastor
The Church on the Way
Van Nuys, California.

COME TO THE VINEYARD

This is my favorite time of year in the vineyard—the waning days of winter.

It is still only mid-February, but in the short winters of California's San Joaquin Valley, spring is just around the corner. The ever-lengthening days are already clawing at winter's grip, and it will soon succumb.

It's just after 5:30 in the afternoon, and the long yellow rays of the setting sun have surrendered to violet-tinted shades of pink. Though it was in the 70's earlier today, the evening chill comes quickly. I zip up my coat against the light breeze, pulling the collar up around my neck and thrusting my hands into its pockets.

Lights from distant farmhouses have already begun to twinkle against the subdued landscape, and out of the diaphanous shroud of evening ground fog that obscures the horizon, rows of grapevines curve over the hills and completely surround me.

The vines are all neatly trimmed, their branches gently twisting around the wire strung from the posts that stand as sentinels beside each vine. The labor of winter brings surrealistic order to the vineyard. Should anything in God's creation be so tightly clipped and neatly arranged?

The vineyard is at rest, waiting patiently the glory of springtime and another season of fruitfulness. I guess that's why I like this time of year so. At the moment just before twilight, the wispy fog and the neatly-trimmed rows combine to grant me that marvelous gift of secluded peace. Except for the softened whine of a few cars far away, the only sound I hear is the crunching of dirt clods underfoot.

Only a few months ago the air was filled with dust, voices and churning of tractor engines that mark the frenzied drive of harvest to get the raisins in before the first rain. A few weeks from now those same things will fill the air as the process of fruitfulness starts all over again.

But now it is quiet. And though a glance from a distant farmhouse might lead someone to believe that I am alone, it is not so. I have come here at this time to walk and talk with the Father.

This has been my cherished prayer closet since I was a young boy. It is a sanctuary of greater reverence than I've known in any cathedral built by human hands. No place on earth more quickly draws me to him, because it is here that we first met, and here we have met so often. This is where I learned to walk with God—to hear his voice and surrender my life to his pleasure.

**No place on earth
more quickly draws me to him,
because it is here that we first met, and
here we have met so often.**

This is my father's vineyard—a 35-acre ranch in the heart of California's Central Valley. My father is a second-generation grape farmer and has for almost all of his 65 years lived within a mile of this very spot. The farthest he ever traveled, interestingly enough, left him in another vineyard in northeastern France where he was wounded in battle just before New Year's Day, 1945.

After the war he purchased the farm next to the one on which he was raised. This vineyard became his tool— not only to provide for his family but more importantly to also teach his four sons about God and his ways. I've learned more about God in this vineyard than in all my years of Bible training and study.

I learned from the lessons Dad taught us, lessons he always backed with the obedience of his own life. I learned about the cycles of the seasons, of God's faithfulness, of overcoming adversity, and of surrendering to his will. Most of Dad's lessons came straight from God's Word, but many others came from his personal observations and encouragement.

I also learned from my own budding relationship with God. In my long walks, usually at dawn or dusk, I read his Word and learned to speak to God, telling him my deepest secrets. Eventually I began to hear him respond—simple stirrings, gentle insight, deep convictions—the voice of God superimposed over my own thoughts. I could know what was on his heart in the same way I was letting him know what was on mine.

In these rows I also preached my first sermon, at 10 years of age, just over by that muscat vine. Do you see where the branches split to form a natural vee? I propped my Bible between them, and it fell open to Ezekiel 34. I read the words and preached to my dog Penny and the other muscat vines nearby.

It was a child's game to be sure, but something incredible happened that summer morning. The Word became alive in my heart, more so than at any time previous when I had sat down to read it. The words that flowed from my lips, the passion from my heart, were not the doings of a ten-year-old. As I came to realize that, I grew frightened.

What had I touched? It was a presence undeniably distinct from my own. I felt wonderful and foolish all at the same time. I realized how loudly I had spoken, and

though how silly I must have looked acting as a preach-
er in this row of vines. I looked about to make sure no
one had seen me, tucked my Bible inside my shirt, and
wandered back to our farmhouse.

But I couldn't deny that something special had happened, that I had connected with the presence of God in
a way I had not before. I had no designs at the time to
be a pastor, being far more enthralled with the airplanes
that sailed over my head, hoping one day to pilot them.
It was just a game that had unexpectedly taken on a life
all its own. I didn't realize it then, but looking back I
know that was the day my life was indelibly stamped
with an affection for God's Word.

The vineyard has always been my special place, and it
is no wonder to me that when Jesus wanted to reveal the
secrets of the kingdom to his followers he made rich use
of farming illustrations generally, and vineyards most
specifically. No other image offers such a rich source of
instruction, encouragement, and challenge.

The passages of Scripture that deal with vines and
grapes are among my favorite in all of God's Word. I
have not only studied them but lived them, and they
have changed my life. The vineyard of my childhood is
not so very different from those which Jesus walked
through with his disciples. I can almost see him leaning
up against the sturdy trunk of an old vine the wicked
tenants of his Father's vineyard.

One evening in particular, as Jesus faced the longest
night of his life, he wanted to convey to his followers
where to find the rich spring of personal fulfillment and
the keys to living fruitful lives. Where did he take them?
To a vineyard—his Father's vineyard.

Fulfillment and *fruitfulness.* No themes recur more frequently in the vineyard than these, and who among us
is not stirred to our deepest desires by their mere mention? Who doesn't want joy and inner peace deep
enough to take us through any circumstance, and a
sense of success that comes from knowing our lives have

made a difference?

**Who doesn't want joy and inner
peace deep enough to take us through
any circumstance, and a sense of success
that comes from knowing our lives
have made a difference?**

For too many people , however, these qualities remain an elusive dream. Though pursued with fervor they are rarely reached.

Many things in this world promise fullness, and though they may provide a moment of happiness or satisfaction, none of them offers the enduring joy and peace we seek so ardently. And who can be sure they are fruitful, especially in things spiritual? Many of us are not even sure what it means, and most of us can honestly admit we don't think we've found it. We might think we're the only ones to feel that way, but we are not. Even those Christians who try to convince others that they have found the secrets of fulfillment and fruitfulness often prove by their own personal stress, immorality or spiritual emptiness that they are not.

This is especially tragic because Jesus didn't want his followers confused or groping for either one. That's why he took them to a vineyard and invited them to take their places in it.

I have long since left the ranch and moved to the city's edge. My days are filled less with vineyards and more with computers, automobiles and other machinery of our technological society. But somehow these never quite measure up to the lessons that come from the heart of God's own creation. We are organisms not machines, and even our spiritual growth patterns have more in common with the four grape vines I have growing today in my backyard than the computer on which I type.

Before we are completely urbanized, it would serve us well to take a look back to our agrarian roots. Scripture makes such vivid use of the images of plant growth and fruitfulness to teach us about our own spiritual life. Here, with less clutter lying between us and God's creation we can learn the rich lessons he taught about his spiritual vineyard.

Previous trips to my father's vineyard for study and reflection have been alone. Now I invite you to go with me, not to his vineyard, but to a far greater vineyard that belongs to God himself.

Let's go to the vineyard together, you and I. Let's walk the rows with the Father of the vineyard and watch his vines grow and bear fruit. We'll even get to stop, pull back the leaves and be able to see the marvelous fruit he is producing. Listen as he teaches us the lessons of the vineyard and show us the secret of finding the fullness of joy and fruitfulness that he has promised to every believer.

Including you!

1

An Amazing Invitation

I have told you this
so that my joy may be in you
and that your joy may be complete.
JOHN 15:11

It had been the strangest of evenings. They had never seen Jesus so deeply troubled. As he served them a Passover meal he made ominous comments about the bread being his broken body and the wine his spilled blood. He said that from their own number one would betray him and another deny him before the morning sunrise.

He warned them that he was going somewhere they could not go, and he promised them a new companion, another Counselor, who would guide them in his place. He told them not to be afraid, and who ever says that without good reason?

Judas had fled the room earlier for reasons none of the others understood. Now they had left the safe confines of that upper room and were headed in the darkness toward the Garden of Gethsemane. Suddenly Jesus took the conversation in an unforeseen direction.

"I am the true vine."

Eyebrows must have popped up around this little band of men as they looked incredulously at one another. Vines? What did vines have to do with the events of this strange evening?

Perhaps Jesus had spotted a small stand of vines in the garden. I can see him walking over to a grapevine, affectionately taking one of the canes in his hand. He might even have squatted down near its trunk, inviting his disciples to gather around him as he launched into one of the more tender metaphors of his ministry—one reserved only for his closest friends.

He compared himself to a vine, his disciples to branches, and his Father to a gardener. He spoke of their need for pruning so that they could bear even more fruit, and of friends laying down their lives for one another.

Before we take in his words, let's look at his intent in speaking them: "I have told you this so that my joy may be in you and that your joy may be complete." Even in the midst of all the fearful unknowns he had introduced throughout the evening, he promised his followers complete joy.

What an unlikely group to be beneficiaries of such a marvelous promise! Take a look at the men sitting around that honored grapevine. Which of these 11 men deserved it? Four years earlier, which of these would you have chosen to dine with any king, much less the King of Glory on the last night of his life?

None of these men had been invited to state dinners at Herod's palace, and none were likely to be in the future. They weren't outcasts necessarily, but most were nondescript people that you would pass on the street and not give a second thought.

He found some of them at the docks, frustrated fishermen who had spent the night and come up empty. One he found in a tax office, another sitting beneath a fig tree. None were remarkable figures in their community, none had been leaders.

But they had just shared the Passover with the King of Glory on the last night of his earthly life, and now they were being told how they could embrace total fulfillment. Who would have thought such a promise would be given to men like these? Certainly not their friends or neighbors, or the Pharisees.

To this unlikely group of men Jesus promised joy to the fullest measure they could conceive. Their culture had not given it to them, and that is not surprising. Cultures only reward a sliver of people with success, and it usually comes to those people with the right abilities, backgrounds, breaks, or achievements.

There's much we don't know of these disciples, but one thing we do know: These are not the kind of people who are supposed to find fullness of joy. They were ordinary people who at times demonstrated the same weaknesses we do—anger, jealousy, greed, and incredible thick-headedness. Though the world only offered them lives of quiet desperation, Jesus extended to them an amazing invitation to absolute joy.

**Though the world only offered them
lives of quiet desperation, Jesus
extended to them an amazing
invitation to absolute joy.**

This is the reason he paused in that small vineyard on the way to the olive groves in Gethsemane; to teach these men how to embrace joy at a level far deeper than their circumstances would ever allow. He wasn't talking about mere happiness, a temporal feeling of satisfaction that results from favorable circumstances. Such happiness is always fleeting, for it only lasts as long as the current circumstance.

Joy on the other hand has a different source. It springs from an inner sense of fulfillment that reaches to the depths of our being. All is well. God's purpose in our life is being fulfilled. This joy often results in happiness, but it also leads to peace, contentedness, and rest. Because it is produced by God's work inside us, true joy is impervious to any change of circumstances.

I have seen joy radiate from people who are in the midst of sacrifice and great loss. It is not a contrived facial expression, but a spring that bubbles up from inside, often in the face of the very circumstances they are enduring.

Our discovery of joy that is real is at the heart of the lesson of the vineyard. You may seem as unlikely a candidate as the 11 men that surrounded Jesus in that garden, and unless you are convinced that the same offer is yours you will never pursue it with the fervency necessary to apprehend it.

I've met many people who cannot believe that such a rich inheritance is theirs. They all have the same hollow glare in their pain-filled eyes. They all ask the same questions: "What hope do I have of ever being happy? Can God help me find the same fulfillment in Christ that you have?" Some were brought to that point through years of abuse and torment, others through willful sin or after years of disappointed pursuit of spirituality. They had not been able to find the God who could fulfill them with his joy.

One of these people came to me very recently. Judy had been rejected by everyone who had ever been close to her, from her birth parents to her adopted parents. She was a real-life Cinderella, but without the carriage and glass slipper. She believed in God, but believed that God had made her only to help expose the sins of others. Her own personal pain mattered not a whit to him.

She hadn't come to that conclusion easily—only after her many pleas for healing had seemingly gone unanswered. Everything she tried had failed, and she was left to the bitter throes of a loneliness that could only be temporarily held at bay with wanton bulimia.

Is there any hope for her? Just as importantly, is there

any hope for *you*? Many of you may be reading this book because you have just such a hope. Hold on to it. Your hope today is the most decisive ingredient to the development of your relationship with God tomorrow.

But others of you may be reading this skeptically. You've tried to find a vital friendship with Jesus any number of times, but your experience, like Judy's, may never have lived up to its promise. Let me assure you at the outset that the promises made in the vineyard will certainly come to pass in everyone who believes in the work the Father has done for you. There is no favoritism with him; he loves all his children equally. If his Word is valid only for people who grew up in safe, middle-class homes, it is not the gospel of Jesus Christ. If it's not real for whoever seeks him, then it is a fraud for everyone else.

Jesus offered it not only to the eleven in the garden that evening, but also throughout his ministry to rich young rulers, hardened Pharisees, lonely beggars, and brazen prostitutes. Not all took his offer, but those who did never expressed disappointment with it.

I can't always explain to people why their past attempts have not been successful; for those who want to build their hope by just such an explanation, I'll not be able to help you here. No general answer could cover every possibility.

You will need to forget the past and all its unanswered questions and start fresh in your walk with God. Let the hope of his promise resurge in you, and pursue it even through difficult moments. Finding fullness is not an easy task, and the cost of that relationship is great. You will see the enemies arrayed against your success in that relationship, but the process cannot even begin if you have no hope that God wants to have such a relationship with you, or if you doubt that he is capable of forging it with you.

"Without faith it is impossible to please God, because anyone who comes to him must believe that he exists and that he rewards those who earnestly seek him." Without that hope we won't seek him earnestly enough or long enough to get through all our baggage and discover the joyful Father and his compassionate Son.

But I promise you now: There is no brokenness he cannot mend; no pain he cannot still; no one he does not invite to the fullness of his joy. *He desires a warm friendship with each one of us,* and he wants to speak with a voice that can offer direction and comfort every day.

**There is no brokenness he cannot mend;
no pain he cannot still; no one he does
not invite to the fullness of his joy.**
*He desires a warm friendship
with each one of us.*

That's why he told the story of the vineyard, and why he told it to a group of people about to face the greatest trial of their young lives.

2

THE GENEROUS LANDLORD

The kingdom of heaven is like a landowner
who went out early in the morning to hire men
to work in his vineyard.
MATTHEW 20:1

Jesus begins on familiar ground, "I am the true vine, and my Father is the gardener."

Though his change of subject might have been abrupt, this was not the first time he'd spoken of the vineyard. Many times before his parables had taken them into the vineyard. This, his final lesson, would build on all the others. For us to fully appreciate the depth of John 15, we'll have to depart now and then to visit the other parables and lessons Jesus had already used to embellish his picture of the vineyard.

Nowhere is that more critical than in our understanding of the Father's role in his vineyard. How we perceive the Father is the key to everything we'll learn in the vineyard, so it is here that Jesus begins. Though this is the first time Jesus referred to him as the gardener, the focus on the Father would not have surprised the disciples. Throughout Jesus' ministry they had witnessed the intimate relationship that Jesus shared with his Father.

It could be argued that the most important lesson Jesus impressed on his disciples was not about the kingdom of God, church management or how to hold worship services. In everything he did, Jesus demonstrated how much the Father loved them and how critical it was for them to learn to trust him absolutely in any and every circumstance.

Jesus demonstrated how much the Father loved them and how critical it was for them to learn to trust him absolutely in any and every circumstance.

To drive home that lesson he had told them another parable, probably only a week earlier, identifying the Father as the landlord and owner of the vineyard. This is the groundwork for the tale he now tells. Let us start there, for the gardener he spoke of had already been identified as the landlord of the vineyard.

If it had happened to me, I'd have been incensed!

I wouldn't care if I had agreed earlier to work all day for 40 dollars. When quitting time came, if I stood there and watched my father give the same forty dollars to one of my brothers who had only come for the last hour of work, I'd have been furious.

But my father never did it. Whether he paid us by the hour or by the vines we pruned or the trays we picked, we got paid only for what we worked. If I worked two hours, I got paid two hours. If I pruned 183 vines, that's what I got paid for—no more, no less!

I've gone out at 6:30 in the morning to chase a dust-spewing tractor around the vineyard, picking up raisins and putting them in boxes. It's not too bad starting out, but somewhere after noon the pain intensifies. One hundred and three degrees of searing heat beats down on the back of your neck.

The dust is so thick you feel it grind between your teeth. So much dirt fills your boots that they feel like cement blocks as you lift them one after the other out of the deep powdery dust.

If at that time more workers were hired, I was never disappointed—only grateful for the extra help. I remember those late afternoons when we tried to get the raisins out of an approaching rainstorm. On those days we weren't working toward a specific quitting time—we would be done only when the crop was safe, even if that came after dark. Any extra help was welcome indeed, but I certainly didn't expect them to receive the same pay that I did.

It is exactly that expectation that makes Jesus' parable of the workers in the vineyard (Matthew 20:1-16) such a powerful teaching tool. In his story the landowner goes to the marketplace five different times during the day to hire workers for his vineyard. We are not told why he does this. Was the work pressing before a destroying storm? Was he demonstrating compassion for those who had not found work earlier in the day? Whatever the reason, each time he finds those willing to help, even to the last hour of the day.

At quitting time he instructs his foreman to do something most curious: pay the workers, beginning with the last ones hired and proceeding in reverse order to the first ones. What must the first workers have thought when they saw those who had been hired last receive the amount that they had been promised? I'd have been a bit concerned at first, but like them, I would have been hopeful that I would get more than I was promised. They said nothing until they received their wages.

What a shock when they received only the amount they had been promised! They received the same as those who had only worked an hour and that in the cooler time of late afternoon. Were they ever angry!

"You have made them equal to us who have borne the burden of the work and the heat of the day." I understand exactly how they felt; that's why this parable has not traditionally been among my personal favorites.

This seeming unfairness is exactly why Jesus told the parable. It hits us so hard because we're left with the incomprehensible feeling that those who started early in the day were not treated fairly. What reasonable person would think otherwise?

But that is the very point of the parable. We don't bring our reasonable expectations to God and demand them satisfied. The landowner's actions in this parable were not unfair toward those who were first out in the field, but simply represented generosity to those who had come later.

We don't bring our reasonable expectations to God and demand them satisfied.

Did he not pay the laborers what he had promised them? There is no unfairness here. "Didn't you agree to work for a denarius? Take your pay and go. I want to give the man who was hired last the same as I gave you. Don't I have the right to do what I want with my own money? Or are you envious because I am generous?"

Doesn't God have the right to do whatever he wants in his own vineyard? Doesn't he know best? Can't he be generous with another without inciting my envy? He is the owner of the vineyard. If we're not ready to trust him to that degree, we will find no joy in his vineyard.

Those for whom the landowner would have had the greatest appreciation were those who worked throughout the entire day. He gave more to the others out of compassion for their need, not because they held a greater place in his heart. But their gratefulness, coupled with the complaints of the first workers, reverses the tables. Jesus makes the saddened conclusion, "So the last will be first, and the first will be last.'

The meaning of this parable applies far beyond the way the Father rewards us. It has to do with the way we view *him* in our lives. Is he ours to control, or are we his to command? Those who started the day first in the Father's heart ended it last, because in their own greed they judged the landowner as unfair even though he had given them exactly what they had agreed to.

If we're going to find fulfillment in the life of Jesus we have got to have a good understanding of who's who in his vineyard. Only as we embrace God's place as the gardener and Jesus' as the vine will we know how to respond to him as branches.

I never had a problem with knowing who was who in my dad's vineyard. Throughout the restlessness of my adolescent years, I had many occasions to second-guess his ideas and decisions. But one area in which I never questioned him was the vineyard. In my eyes he was the master farmer and I his worker. Whatever he said went. He knew best.

Regretfully, the same hasn't always been true of my relationship with my heavenly Father. Whenever things didn't go right, this junior Job would plead his case before God. Since I knew God wasn't unfair, I assumed he didn't have all the facts he needed, and I was always happy to share some of mine with him. Even though I knew God, I did not trust him *as* God.

I have seen God do many things that defy my reasonable expectations, extending grace to others in ways that didn't seem fair in light of what I had gone through. I have resisted his work, complained at my perceptions of his inactivity, and railed at his judgments.

There have been times when I have spent the bulk of my prayer life trying to counsel God to resolve my situation in the only way I could imagine a loving God doing so. But that only shows the limits of my imagination, not evidence that the Father lacks power, compassion, or fairness.

When I told my dad about such conversations with the Almighty he would shake his head in disbelief. "Who are you to talk to God that way?" he would ask.

He knew something about the Father that I have only since come to fully appreciate. He is over all; he is not to be *challenged* but *followed*. Though we can always ask him for more insight, charging him with dereliction of duty will get us nowhere.

We will not always understand why God does what he does, but we must learn to trust him enough to endorse his plans for us instead of trying to get him to fulfill ours. If we're not willing to let God extend his grace in ways more marvelous than we understand, we risk disqualifying ourselves from his joy.

I have since come to trust God as the owner of the vineyard in which I am planted. Rare are the moments now that my prayers challenge God's working in my life. Letting my Father be the owner of the vineyard brings rest inside even when circumstances rage without. I always note how much God has changed my heart when I'm caught in a crisis with someone who hasn't yet learned that we are only branches in his vineyard.

They say things like "Why didn't God prevent this?" or "How could he just sit by and watch it happen?" Who's to say he did? Why do we trust our personal limited perspective in a situation more than we trust that God is at work by means other than we would perceive or prefer?

The problem with persistently demanding that God's actions satisfy our own desires is that it will eventually destroy the trust so essential to our relationship with him. The people of Israel did the same thing, and were chastised for it strongly:

"Woe to him who quarrels with his Maker....Does the clay say to the potter, 'What are you making?'" (Isaiah 45:9).

Most people don't evidence such frustration with God all the time. I see it mostly when crises and confusing circumstances hit. Then I clearly see the anguish that hides beneath the surface of their otherwise-contented spiritual lives. At that point they can tick off a list of their disappointments with God that stretches back over many years. If an unwillingness to trust God is present in a crisis, you can be sure it adversely impacts your relationship with him at many other times as well.

Precisely at moments of crisis is where our trust is needed most. If we can hold on to it then, it will give us the peace and security we need to draw close to God. Without it, we'll shove him away at arm's length and the resulting circumstances will only seem to confirm our conclusion that he is not treating us fairly.

Trusting God unquestioningly is a choice of faith that we all must make. What are you going to believe: your interpretation of events, or God's revealed character attested to by thousands of his people throughout history? In any situation you can know instantly what you're trusting. Our own perspectives will leave us frustrated and discouraged, eventually trapping us in despair. In contrast, whenever we choose to trust God, our hearts will fill with peace and security. I am in his hands and therefore I am safe.

**Whenever we choose to trust God,
our hearts will fill with peace
and security. I am in his hands
and therefore I am safe.**

In the advantage of hindsight, I can look back even to those moments when I was disappointed with God's working in my life and fully affirm that God had something better in mind. He has always been faithful to me, seeking the highest good for my life even when it was beyond my ability to understand.

People insecure in the love of the Father will always blame God in circumstances, only to justify themselves. "I'm doing my part, what's wrong with him?" When Paul wrote his letter to the Romans he expressed his absolute trust in God, stating that the issue of the Father's heart toward him was settled on the cross. "He who did not spare his own Son...how will he not also, along with him, graciously give us all things?" (8:32)

No greater proof of love could be given. If he gave the most costly thing he could give; wouldn't he give us anything else we need? Relationship with the Father begins with that trust, that's why it begins at the foot of the cross.

Now we no longer blame God in our circumstances to justify ourselves. We instead justify God, "He is right concerning everything;" and we blame ourselves, "I'm just not sure what he's got in mind in this circumstance."

"Don't I have the right to do what I want with my own money?" The conclusion of the parable of the generous landlord is haunting in its simplicity: Let God be God. A marvelous moment occurs in the life of a believer when he finally realizes that he cannot judge the Father's character by his present circumstances. We simply don't understand enough to do so.

Instead, judge your circumstances by what you know to be true of the Father's love for you. It may not be evident to you that God is involved in the circumstance you're going through, but you can know he is, because he is always loving and faithful.

3

THE TENDER
CARETAKER

Sing about a fruitful vineyard: I, the Lord,
watch over it; I water it continually. I guard it
day and night so that no one may harm it.
ISAIAH 27:2,3

In the last chapter I risked confirming what many people fear most about cultivating a personal relationship with God: The thought of God lording over the vineyard as its owner didn't stir in them blissful thoughts of trust. Instead, it only sounded like a common refrain—might makes right! God is just bigger than we are, so all we can do is blindly trust him even when he seems unfair.

Such thoughts are particularly common to people who have felt powerless in the face of someone else's demands on their life. A school bully—or even more painful, a domineering father or other authority figure—can teach this lesson all too well. They have not known authority apart from its misuse, taking advantage of people for their own gain, and discarding them when they are no longer a source of pleasure. 'Might makes right' to them means that the strong get their way because everyone else is helpless against them. But nothing could be more wrong when applied to the Master of the vineyard.

A young couple I know have a chronically ill child who has been that way since birth. They may never see him grow to adulthood. Despite their earnest pleadings, God has not as yet done one visible thing to improve the health of this child. Day after day they watch him suffer in pain and in the limitations that his condition forces upon him, waiting for what they perceive to be his impending death, confused about God's intentions for them.

I hurt every time I pray for them because in my own limited way I understand their feelings. Our own first-born child had a severe case of jaundice. Every day we bundled up our fragile infant against winter's penetrating cold and took her back to the hospital, where they drew blood from her tender feet. Our days-old daughter screamed in pain.

We watched those first five days as her blood count continued to climb. The doctor told us that if the count didn't drop tomorrow, we would have to put her back in the hospital. Even though her condition wasn't life-threatening and relatively speaking her pain was minimal, I remember how frustrated I was driving back from the hospital that afternoon wondering why we couldn't just take our daughter home and enjoy her like everyone else.

The next day her count was down, and soon our trips to the hospital ended. I can't tell you how grateful we were to God. When I think of this other couple, and multiply my five-day frustration by eight years, I begin to get a glimpse of their distress. To them, hearing that God needs to be trusted because he is bigger than anyone else may not be all that comforting.

For them to walk in the fullness of the kingdom, they must come to know God at a deeper level than just beholding his awesome command over the affairs of the vineyard. As the landowner we can understand his authority and our accountability to him. He is God, after all, and we certainly can expect no less.

To stop there, however, will lead us to a severely distorted picture of God. We not only need to see the authority he holds, but how he *exercises* that authority. This landowner is also the gardener—one who takes care of his own vineyard. Isaiah paints a touching portrait of God as he cares for his vineyard with great compassion. He watches over it. He waters it continually. He guards it day and night so no one can harm it.

The word translated "gardener" or "husbandman" in John 15 carries the meaning of one intimately involved in the growth and nurturing of the vines. This, Jesus said, depicts the Father's role in the garden. He is not just the awesome, majestic Creator of all, but also a God of gentle tenderness who treats the objects of his creation with overwhelming love. The picture of the vineyard draws together both aspects of God's nature and presents them to us in a dynamic tension that makes God wholly attractive. He cares for each branch with intimate care.

**The picture of the vineyard draws
together both aspects of God's nature
and presents them to us in a
dynamic tension that makes
God wholly attractive.**

I have seen the reflection of that care in my earthly father's eyes toward his own vineyard. He was part of a passing generation of family farmers. He cared for his own vines, refusing to buy more land than he could farm himself. He could never have been a manager of a farming conglomerate. If you were to pass by his farm, he (or his children) would be the ones you would see out in the morning frost—pruning the vines, or driving his tractor through a moving cloud of dust.

Recently he retired and sold his farm because he would not stay on the land beyond his ability to farm it. Many farmers hire out the work to others, or even rent out the entire vineyard to someone else's care. They still live on the farm, but only as landlords. But not my father. He did not relish hired hands in his vineyard. He only hired others for the work he could not possibly do himself, and that with great apprehension.

No one he ever hired met his exacting standards. That wasn't because he thought of himself as the world's greatest farmer, but because he knew that no one else would care for his vineyard as much as he did. When he did have to hire, he preferred his family and friends. Maybe they would share his concern.

I've seen the disappointed look in his eye when he saw raisins carelessly strewn on the ground after someone had turned the trays or rolled them. The person paid by the number of trays doesn't care whether a bunch falls off or not. His wages will be affected if he stops his momentum to pick it up.

I've also felt his pain when he gazed at a vine I had carelessly pruned. In my haste to race my brothers to the end of the row, I had cut off too many good canes. There were not enough left for the vine to reach its full potential in the year ahead. I remember my father's patience in telling us to slow down, training us to do a better job.

But no lesson was more powerful than the fact that I had let him down. Somehow my treatment of that vine had hurt *him*. I could see it in his eyes, even though he demonstrated no anger. I looked at the good canes lying useless on the ground at my feet. If only I could have glued them back on...

Let me risk mixing metaphors because Jesus illustrates this exact point with a different agricultural analogy. Perhaps he knew that we could understand care directed to animals more easily than grapevines. Even in this day, when scientists tell us our plants will grow better if we talk nice to them, we still don't see people weeping over the death of their favorite houseplant. But if you've ever had a pet you deeply loved, you'll understand the shepherd's love for his sheep.

> *I am the good shepherd. The good shepherd lays down his life for the sheep. The hired hand is not the shepherd who owns the sheep. So when he sees the wolf coming, he abandons the sheep and runs away. Then the wolf attacks the flock and scatters it. The man runs away because he is a hired hand and cares nothing for the sheep.*
>
> JOHN 10:11-13

Here's an interesting shepherd. In the midst of danger he willingly lays down his life for the sheep, risking his own to keep them safe. That's how deeply Christ loves his own. No hired hand would show the same care; he will labor only until the pain or risk exceeds the quantity of his paycheck—then he's off to find safer pastures.

David risked his own life against a bear and a lion on two separate occasions to rescue his sheep. Farming with an eye only to the bottom line would never even consider such a sacrifice. How could anyone think to risk a human life for a sheep? How about a God who would trade his life for yours?

How could anyone think to risk a human life for a sheep? How about a God who would trade his life for yours?

This is the gardener in whose vineyard you have been planted. His vine is his own Son, and each branch another son or daughter. He loves them more than any other ever could. When I ask someone to surrender to the landlord of the vineyard, this is the one to whom they surrender—the God of tender lovingkindness and compassion, whose mercies never fail.

I can't explain to the young couple why their son suffers so; and though I understand their pain, it is truly misdirected if the Father is the source of it. He loves them and their son, and though I can't explain his seeming inactivity of the past, I know it is not complicity.

If I understand their pain, how much more does he? God has not hung back indifferent to their prayers or their pain, but has labored over the suffering as well. He wants to redeem their situation, bringing glory out of pain, but to see it they will have to let go of their mistaken conclusions and trust him.

Certainly it won't be easy. Disappointment and hurt can be difficult obstacles to overcome. But the father even knows that. That's why he pictures himself coming to us with such tenderness. Maybe, just maybe, it will sink through one day, and we'll give up fighting just long enough to see the incredible love of the one who holds us in his hands.

The gardener is fully capable of taking any branch, no matter how wounded, and putting it back together again. This may not mean a quick fix. It may take awhile, but the Father has grace enough to forgive our failures, and strength enough to transform any crisis.

The Father has grace enough to forgive our failures, and strength enough to transform any crisis.

Even when other laborers worked for my father, he kept a sharp eye on their work. Long after they had gone home to rest for the day, my father would walk the rows. He was always the last one out of the vineyard. He would pick grapes that others had missed, scoop up raisins that had been spilled on the ground, and find canes that had come unwrapped from the wire (and tie them up again).

I have seen God do the same thing in the lives of his

people. No matter what we endure, no matter how much others might have failed us, he wants to be the last one to touch every area of our lives. Cleaning up from our mistakes and the abuses of others, he can bring fruitfulness out of the most dire circumstances.

The story of Joseph is not meant to be a unique one in The Father's kingdom. It reveals his heart for all of his children. The envy of Joseph's brothers led him to be sold as a slave in Egypt. There we still find God, working to fulfill his plan for Joseph even though others meant him great harm. Later, when Joseph was falsely accused because of the integrity of his heart, God even used his unjust jail sentence as a stepping-stone to the highest rank in Pharaoh's kingdom.

Can you believe him to do the same in your own life? It is this kind of trust that allows me to release so much significant ministry to people in the congregation where I serve. I used to worry about people making mistakes. Not every need would be met perfectly; often the wrong thing would be said or the right thing left unsaid. How greatly someone could be damaged, I would think. But not any longer. If they are looking to the Father, he will always be the last one to move through their lives. He will heal hurts and override failures, using both as greater stepping-stones to growth.

Now that's a gardener you can trust completely!

4

THE FAITHFUL PROVIDER

Then the Father will give you...
JOHN 15:16

In many ways my father's care for his vineyard mirrors the way the heavenly Father cares for us. But there is one aspect of his care for the vineyard that my father could never duplicate.

God can superintend every detail of his vineyard, monitor every circumstance, and overcome any enemy of growth. Though my father did as much as he could for his vines—irrigating when the rains were insufficient and fertilizing to enrich the soil—he was not always able to overcome all the forces of nature. He was as much a victim of the elements as each vine in his vineyard.

One day I watched him as rain fell on his freshly picked crop, bringing total destruction to a year's worth of labor. It's not supposed to rain in September, and if he could have stopped it, he would have. I've seen other vineyards wiped out by a late freeze in spring. If the vines have already budded, a freeze will destroy the grapes. Though the vine will grow and look as lush as ever, it will be completely bare of grapes.

Paul recognized that in both vineyards, physical and spiritual, though our own efforts are limited, God's are not: "Neither he who plants nor he who waters is anything, but only God, who makes things grow" (1 Corinthians 3:7). He is not only the caretaker of the vineyard, but he is also Master over all creation and the force behind every stage of our growth.

He is not only the caretaker of the vineyard, but he is also Master over all creation and the force behind every stage of our growth.

He not only cares for us, but he has the power to change any circumstance we face. He can give us whatever we need to flourish, and he has power enough to overcome obstacles set against us. Throughout Jesus' story of the vineyard the Father continually hovers in the background. He is not just the gardener who prunes, but the loving Father who provides everything his children need.

That connection would have been especially meaningful to Jesus' hearers in that upper room because of the role that vineyards played in the Old Testament. In Genesis, God called Joseph a fruitful vine, and from that point on the vineyards of Israel acted as special symbols of God's provision and care.

Why a vineyard? Why not a wheat field?

Remember that the Israelites began as a nomadic people. Vines to them were unthinkable. Unlike wheat, vines aren't planted in the spring and harvested a few months later. It takes five years to bring a newly planted vine into full production. When God promised his people vineyards he was telling them he would settle them down in safety long enough to partake of their fruit. His work in them was not just for the moment. The Father's perspective encompassed not just the present, but the whole of their lives.

The Father's perspective encompassed not just the present, but the whole of their lives.

Israel's vineyards became the symbol of the longevity of God's provision and care, his promise to allow them to settle in one place for an extended period of time and be at rest. When they settled in Canaan they became the beneficiary even of vineyards they hadn't planted—a sign of God's abundance:

> *When the Lord your God brings you into the land he swore to your fathers, to Abraham, Isaac and Jacob, to give you—a land with large, flourishing cities you did not build, houses filled with all kinds of good things you did not provide, wells you did not dig, and vineyards and olive groves you did not plant.*
>
> DEUTERONOMY 6:10,11

When they returned from the exile in Babylon, God reassured them that they would once again be planted in Canaan and have the chance to plant vineyards again, a sign of the enduring protection God would extend to them:

> *They will live there in safety and will build houses and plant vineyards; they will live in safety when I inflict punishment on all their neighbors who maligned them. Then they will know that I am the Lord their God.*
>
> EZEKIEL 28:26

When God blessed his people you could see it in their vineyards. He promised them weather tailor-made for their crops if they would keep him first in their hearts: "I will send rain on your land in its season, both autumn and spring rains, so that you may gather in your grain, new wine and oil" (Deuteronomy 11:14).

Conversely, when God removed his provision as an act of judgment against those who had forsaken him, that too was reflected in their vineyards. Without his involvement their security was lost, and along with it their provision and their joy:

> You trample on the poor and force him to give you grain. Therefore, though you have built stone mansions, you will not live in them; though you have planted lush vineyards, you will not drink their wine.
>
> AMOS 5:11

> The earth is defiled by its people; they have disobeyed the laws, violated the statutes and broken the everlasting covenant. Therefore a curse consumes the earth; its people must bear their guilt. Therefore earth's inhabitants are burned up, and very few are left. The new wine dries up and the vine withers; all the merrymakers groan.
>
> ISAIAH 24:5-7

There are not many things so desperate-looking as a withered vineyard. When vines die it is not like a corn crop falling victim to a drought. No matter how great the damage to the corn, it is still only one year's loss. Next year's corn can be replanted and a full crop harvested. Not so with the vine. If it is destroyed, crops are wiped out for years to come. No sight is more forlorn than rows and rows of vines, shriveled and withered, the leaves blackened and the canes drooping to the ground.

But even after such days of judgment God promised to restore his people, bringing them back to the security and provision that he had always desired them to have. Once again, their grape crop specifically was singled out as a sign of this restoration:

> *The Lord has sworn by his right hand and by his mighty arm: "Never again will I give your grain as food for your enemies, and never again will foreigners drink the new wine for which you have toiled; but those who harvest it will eat it and praise the Lord, and those who gather the grapes will drink it in the courts of my sanctuary."*
>
> ISAIAH 62:8,9

Even in his prophecies of coming destruction, Isaiah promised Israel she would once again be a fruitful vineyard:

> *In the days to come Jacob will take root, Israel will bud and blossom and fill all the world with fruit.*
>
> ISAIAH 27:6

So it goes through much of the Old Testament. Firmly set in the minds of the disciples as they gathered around Jesus in that vineyard on their last night together was the significance of the grapevine as a symbol of God's provision. The Lord's blessing and discipline were measured in Israel's vineyards and so was his withholding of that provision when their hearts wandered after false gods.

The disciples already knew God as more than a farmer at the whim of rogue storms and swarms of leaf-eating insects. He is God, behind the scenes in every situation. But this wouldn't mean to them that just because God is able to control circumstances he correspondingly does so to ensure for us a life of ease. You don't have to walk with God long to see that even though he could do so, he does not override every adverse or painful circumstance in our lives.

Some people, not understanding this, see every moment of need or disease as proof that God either doesn't care for them or is powerless to change their circumstances. The connection between righteousness and external provision seems to be far closer in the Old Testament than in the New. God used that connection as a demonstration of the spiritual realities that exist. When we seek God, he gives us life. When we turn away from him, the death caused by our sin is released to work against us.

But even in the Old Testament this relationship was not absolute. Consider the story of Job, whose great calamities are depicted not as punishment for any unrighteousness, but only as an onslaught of Satan to try to destroy Job's faith. Such things happen in a world entangled in sin and hostile to the God who created it, where Satan himself is the prince of this age.

In the New Testament the priority of spiritual life is shown to be inside us. Peace and joy abound for the believer, often in defiance of the circumstances they face and not because of them. While the message of the Old Testament could easily be misunderstood as "Follow God and avoid trouble," the New Testament makes it clear that to follow God will bring you adversity.

Peace and joy abound for the believer, often in defiance of the circumstances they face and not because of them.

"We must go through many hardships to enter the kingdom of God" was a word of encouragement that Paul and Barnabus brought to the early church. How many of us would consider that much of an encouragement?

It would only be such if those hearing it were already

encountering great difficulties and pain. Instead of using hardships as evidence that God cannot be trusted, they discover that without such hardships access to the kingdom is denied. This doesn't mean we have to suffer to earn access, but rather that our fleshly nature is often confronted and overcome only in moments of adversity.

Two streams of understanding must flow together here. Though God often chooses to be our provider *through* difficulties and not *from* them, that in no way diminishes his power to override them when he so desires. The New Testament shows God doing both.

Though God often chooses to be our provider *through* difficulties and not *from* them, that in no way diminishes his power to override them when he so desires.

Jesus submitted to the hostility of those who nailed him to a cross, but only days earlier he had confronted the false religion of the Pharisees. Once he suspended the storm that threatened the disciples on the Sea of Galilee, but there's no indication that he did the same with any other storm they faced.

The early church seemed to see no difference in God's provision whether he was transporting Philip supernaturally to Azotus after speaking to the Ethiopian or riding the waves with Paul adrift in the open seas because of a shipwreck. The same God works in different ways.

Certainly God is able to change any of our circumstances and even invites our requests to do so. But if he chooses not to remove our adversity, we are to rest in knowing that adversity is as much a part of our growing as is rest. It is not the most enjoyable part certainly, but it is almost always the most effective part.

It takes an entire year to produce one crop in a vineyard. During this time there are periods of rest and hardship, and all of them are necessary for the fruit to develop and ripen. The same is true for us. We need times of rest and challenge to bear the fruit of God's character in our lives. In each of the four seasons there are hostile elements that the vine endures.

In winter the vine must be pruned to ensure enough strength for a fruitful harvest many months away. In spring, freezing temperatures or hail can strip the vine of its young leaves and budding grape bunches. The heat of summer and the assault of various pests during that time can put so much stress on the vine that the fruit will not ripen. During the harvest, unseasonable rain can cause mildew and rot that will ruin the crop at the end of it all.

All of these pose a significant threat to the vine. They have the potential to destroy it, but at the same time many of these hardships in the right measure actually assist the maturing of the fruit. The good farmer knows which hardships to fight against on the vine's behalf and the ones that are necessary for the vine to be fruitful. So does the Father with us.

As we grow in the vineyard we can trust God as our provider. Regardless of the circumstances, he is as able to change *them*, as he is to change *us* through them. The choice is his, not ours. Our response should not be, "If God loved me this wouldn't be happening," but rather, "Because he loves me even in this, what is he doing in my life greater than I can see?"

A poignant line from David is a good encouragement to us all: "Those who know your name will trust in you, for you, Lord, have never forsaken those who seek you" (Psalm 9:10). To know God's name is to know the faithfulness of his character and the endless depths of his love. Those who know that fact will put their trust in him.

If you're having a difficult time trusting the Father in the circumstances you face today, it's only because you need to know him better. And he wants nothing more.

5

A Peek at God's Priority

He cuts off every branch in me that bears no fruit,
while every branch that does bear fruit he prunes
so that it will be even more fruitful.
John 15:2

There's nothing a farmer likes to do more than peek.

Throughout the development of his crop, he's always peeking to see how it's coming along and how big he can anticipate the harvest to be.

To this day, anytime between the first budding and the final day of harvest, I can ask my father, ``How does the crop look?'' and without hesitation he always has an answer.

"About average," or, "Looks like 15 percent above normal."

Even when the grape bunches are smaller than the eraser on my pencil, he's already seen them, looked at how many grapes fill those bunches and how many bunches hang from each vine. That all takes some serious peeking.

So when I think of a grape farmer the image that

comes most quickly to mind is when he reaches into a vine with both hands, pulling back the leaves and peeking into every nook and cranny. He is as delighted by every bunch he sees as a child under a Christmas tree finding brightly wrapped packages with his name on them.

This peeking continues even in days after the harvest—just in case one of those gifts had been missed by the harvesters. There is nothing more important to a farmer than the fruit growing in his field. After all, why else plant a vineyard?

In Jesus' lesson on the vineyard he tells us that his Father is no different. Nine times in his brief sermon reference is made to fruit or fruitfulness (John 15:1-17). Everything the Father does in his vineyard is geared to making each branch on the vine fruitful.

If a branch doesn't bear fruit he cuts it off. No sense wasting the vine's energy on that which will not bear fruit. If a branch *does* bear fruit he cuts it too—not *off,* but he prunes it *up* so that it can be even more fruitful.

Fruit, fruit, fruit! That is the Father's priority, and unless we come to share it we will be forever frustrated with the Lord's dealing in our lives. Unfortunately, we haven't all come to the kingdom of God with that same priority.

Fruit, fruit, fruit!
That is the Father's priority,
and unless we come to share it we
will be forever frustrated with the Lord's
dealing in our lives.

Some of us came to the kingdom because we were scared. God offered us security in the face of our fears. Surely, we think, there is nothing more important to God than making sure my circumstances never again make me feel insecure.

Some of us came to God in a moment of crisis. He

offered answers to rescue us. Surely, we think, there is nothing more important to God than making sure I am never in need again.

Some of us came to God out of great anguish and guilt for our own sins. He forgave us and promised cleansing. Surely, we think, there is nothing more important to God than protecting me from any temptation that will cause me to sin.

Some of us came to God brokenhearted by the misery of circumstances we had endured. He was a strong tower and healed the hurts that raged in our souls. Surely, we think, there is nothing more important to God than making sure I am happy and never hurt again.

Think again! Is God's greatest priority our feelings of security, safety, or happiness? Many people, confident that it is, find themselves in great confusion when those expectations are not satisfied.

Here is the cause: God has one priority in your life—to make you fruitful. Our priority, however, is often not so noble. We would much rather be happy or at the very least comfortable. Since God's priority will carry the day, as long as we hold to any objective but fruitfulness we'll find ourselves in continual conflict with God's work in us.

For some this talk of fruitfulness may seem a far cry from our early discussion of fulfillment. "That your joy may be full" may seem to have little in common with "that you bear fruit," but a farmer knows that they are directly linked. Fruit only results from fullness. And the Father knows that only out of fruitfulness do we find true joy.

What is best for the vine's life is also best for its fruitfulness, for fruit is simply the overflow of life. Healthy vines produce fruit; stressed vines do not. A vine poorly pruned, poorly nourished, or encountering a severe lack of water will cast off its fruit in order to keep itself alive for future seasons.

On the other hand, no vine left to itself will be fruitful; it will instead become a sprawling mass of fruitless leaves and branches. Attacked by insects and weakened by lack of care, there will not be enough life to bear any fruit. Neither would we be able to bear fruit if God allowed us every one of our ambitions and every quest for comfort.

Neither would we be able to bear fruit if God allowed us every one of our ambitions and every quest for comfort.

That's why the Father trains and disciplines his vines. Though it causes some rough going in the short term, he wants them to know the fullness of joy that comes from being fruitful.

To accept the Father's priority of fruitfulness we have to be willing to endure temporal difficulties at times. Jesus demonstrated that to his disciples when he approached Jerusalem for the last time. Though his disciples didn't understand, he told them that the hour for his death had come. Then in what appears to be a spontaneous burst of emotion, we see the battle Jesus fought.

"Now my heart is troubled, and what shall I say? 'Father, save me from this hour'?" Isn't that the cry that springs most easily to mind when we encounter trouble? It also did for him. Should he pray that way, he asked his disciples? Certainly our Lord wanted to forgo the pain, but he chose something better.

"No, it was for this very reason I came to this hour. Father, glorify your name!" (John 12:23-28). Wonderfully for us he chose the better response. Instead of crying out for his own salvation, he put God's glory first. He sought God's glory over his own comfort, and in so doing showed us the way to be fruitful.

In a study which our fellowship shared through the book of John, we came to this very passage on one of the most painful Sunday mornings I've known. The day before a mother of four young children, the wife of one of the leaders in our congregation, died most unexpectedly on her thirty-fifth birthday. She seemed perfectly healthy up to a week before, when she suddenly had a convulsion. What doctors originally thought was an aneurysm turned out to be a very rare blood disease that brought her life to a swift conclusion. Many in our congregation were only finding out that morning.

And what shall we say? "Father save us from this hour"? Wouldn't we all want to pray just that? Don't let bad things happen to us. But our prayer must be, "Father, be glorified even in this moment." That prayer releases God to take the most painful of our circumstances and use them for his glory.

That does not mean he orchestrates our pain, or delights in our suffering. Nothing could be farther from the truth. I don't think God killed that young mother, any more than he planned for Stephen to be stoned by an angry mob. Though both events were in the context of his will, acts of destruction are the work of darkness. God chose to use them for his purposes. I cannot tell you why the woman died, but I can tell you that even from her husband's own lips God's faithfulness has been affirmed again and again. As we shared earlier, his love is big enough to contain even a horrible circumstance such as this.

That does not mean he orchestrates our pain, or delights in our suffering. Nothing could be further from the truth.

A God who is preoccupied with our personal convenience would never have allowed persecution to scatter the church in Judea, or Paul to battle a thorn in the flesh, or James to die by Herod' sword. Obviously God is motivated at a level far higher than our personal convenience. Through all of our adversities he seeks a deeper fruitfulness and uses our circumstances for greater redemption.

He has not promised us circumstances that guarantee our comfort. Instead his priority is to make us *fruitful,* and we all know that the greatest fruit is often born of the most intense struggles. Great promises in God's kingdom come with great responsibility. Too often we emphasize the former and ignore the latter.

As much as God delights in blessing his children, the intent of that blessing is so that we might be a blessing to others. From Abraham on down God invites people to blessing so that through them he might make his blessings available to all the nations of the earth.

As much as God delights in blessing his children, the intent of that blessing is so that we might be a blessing to others.

Israel had a difficult time keeping that perspective. They misunderstood God's blessing as privilege alone and not as a responsibility to share God's goodness with those around them. Let us not make the same mistake. We should always be looking for ways God wants to use us as a means to bless others.

The only priority that drives the Master of the vineyard is to bring us to fruitfulness. He will do whatever it takes to make that happen. That's also why the farmer peeks so often. He is not just estimating the crop, but also assessing how that crop is doing. Is it maturing? Are there any pests, mildew, or diseases attempting to destroy that harvest? Is there anything he can do to help the vine to greater fruitfulness?

Everything a farmer does is linked to this peeking. You don't grow grapes in the same way you build a bookcase. It's not a matter of following well-prescribed steps within a controlled environment: Cut this, glue that, sand here. Growing a crop is a dynamic process, demanding constant adjustment to an ever-changing environment. There is no schedule to follow that will work successfully each year. You have to observe the vine and its needs in light of the current weather and circumstances that impact the vineyard.

During the year the vines will need pruning and training. Weeds will need to be pulled and pests sprayed. At the right times the vines will need to be irrigated. No fixed schedule suffices; each year is too different, each too unique. So it is with God and us: He watches over the fruit growing in our lives, carefully tending to its development and thereby ensuring the harvest that is to come. Nothing delights his heart more than finding his vines spilling over with fruit. That's the reason he plants them and nourishes them. Consequently, there is no greater demonstration of worship or honor than finding our way into a fruitful Christian life.

This requires that we follow the same path Jesus blazed. In whatever circumstances you face, pray as Jesus did. Forsake your desire for personal comfort and submit each moment to God's design: "Father, glorify your name." In God's vineyard, fruitfulness is not optional. It will take us to some dark valleys, but even in our most difficult moments he will still be there, giving us abundance in the midst of our sacrifice, healing for our hurts, courage in the face of fear, and joy and peace that can flourish even in crisis.

He will still be there, giving us abundance in the midst of our sacrifice, healing for our hurts, courage in the face of fear, and joy and peace that can flourish even in crisis.

Being fruitful will also lead us to some impressive

peaks. There is no greater exhilaration in a believer's life than sensing the Father's delight when he pulls back the leaves and sees his fruit growing from our branch.

6

WHAT DO YOU MEAN, FRUITFUL?

This is to my Father's glory,
that you bear much fruit,
showing yourselves to be my disciples.
JOHN 15:8

Imagine you've arrived at my father's ranch during the high days of harvest. "Sit here," my father tells you, "while I get you some of the fruit of my vineyard." Immediately you picture a bulging bunch of vine-ripened grapes, their green color dusted with the faintest touch of gold from the sugar packed inside. You can almost taste the sweet juice exploding in your mouth with each bite.

What if, however, when he returns he brings you a bowl of boiled grape leaves, or a plate of stir-fried vine bark?

You would be shocked! Everyone knows that you don't grow a grapevine for leaves or bark. Though a local ethnic dish is prepared in cooked grape leaves, no one around here has any doubt about the fruit of the grapevine: those round succulent grapes that hang in bunches from the vine. Chew on some leaves if you like, or even the canes. But after you've bitten into the grapes you'll be satisfied by nothing else on the vine.

With the same simplicity let us be sure what fruitfulness actually is in the kingdom of God. Throughout the last chapter I talked of fruitfulness—how it is God's one driving passion for his vineyard—but I never precisely defined what that fruit is. Before I do, let me ask you, What do you think spiritual fruit is?

Did you come away from the last chapter having defined with a certainty that you are in fact bearing that fruit to God? If you did and you were right, great! But I find that most people define fruitfulness by the very thing they lack. There's almost a mindset among believers reminiscent of an abused child: Whatever I do isn't good enough!

If I'm effective in leading a Bible study, I'm sure that real fruitfulness lies in bringing new converts to the kingdom. If I'm evangelistically successful, then I'm sure that real fruit lies in practically serving people in need. If I'm serving people in need, I only do it because I can't do the "real" work of the kingdom, which is teaching great numbers of people.

On and on the cycle goes, few of us ever hearing God's delight, "Well done!" We're just not quite sure what it is he really wants of us.

Part of our confusion about fruitfulness stems from our bent to *quantify* everything as a measure of success—number of converts, bodies in pews, churches in the denomination. Certainly our society's penchant for focusing on the bottom line is no help here. Add to that an incomplete view of Scripture's use of fruitfulness and it's no wonder our view is blurred.

The Old Testament uses fruitfulness almost exclusively to refer to having babies—progeny. "Fruitful" is used 13 times in Genesis, and 12 of those times specifically refer to increasing in number, mostly through bearing offspring. From God's first instructions to the animals he created to his promises to the patriarchs, fruitfulness was specifically linked with an increase of numbers.

Only a few references hint at God's deeper view of what it means for us to be fruitful in his kingdom. Psalm 72:3 links fruit with righteousness and Isaiah 32:17 extends that application: "The fruit of righteousness will be peace; the effect of righteousness will be quietness and confidence forever." But perhaps the clearest reference comes in Hosea 10:12: "Sow for yourselves righteousness, reap the fruit of unfailing love, and break up your unplowed ground; for it is time to seek the Lord, until he comes and showers righteousness on you."

Fruit here is seen as an expression of righteousness that comes from the unfailing love of the Father. Here Scripture's definition of fruitfulness deepens beyond a simplistic increase of numbers and deals with the depth of our character.

In the New Testament the tables turn completely. There is only one reference to fruitfulness as expanded numbers(Colossians 1:6), and that passage deals with the fruitfulness of the gospel. When the fruitfulness of *individual* lives is addressed, however, only one definition is used: Fruitfulness is the demonstration of God's transforming power in the character of his people.

Fruitfulness is the demonstration of God's transforming power in the character of his people.

John the Baptist encourages us to "produce fruit in keeping with repentance." In Philippians 1:11 Paul exhorts believers to be "filled with the fruit of righteousness that comes through Jesus Christ—to the glory and praise of God." In Ephesians 5 he contrasts the difference between the fruit of the light (goodness, righteousness, and truth) with the fruitlessness of darkness.

Finally, in Galatians 5:22,23, a passage long revered for its profound simplicity and clarity, he lists the fruits that God desires from his people:

> *The fruit of the Spirit is love, joy, peace, patience, kindness, goodness, faithfulness, gentleness and self-control. Against such things there is no law.*

The first three fruits—love, joy, and peace—are often referred to as blessings that God bestows on his children. He gives us the capacity to love, fills our life with his joy, and gives peace that goes beyond anything we can understand.

The second three fruits define our relationships to other people. Scripture encourages us to be patient with all, to demonstrate kindness in every opportunity we have, and to be a reflection of God's goodness and justice in our actions.

Finally, the last three fruits mark the demeanor of someone who is being transformed by God's kingdom. They are faithful through good times and bad; are gentle in spirit, rather than forcing their will on others; and have self under control, living only to please the one who redeemed them.

There is no need to define these fruits further. Even a child understands what love is, or joy, or what it means to be kind. These are not difficult concepts to understand. They are only difficult to live out daily.

But let's take all these traits together. What would someone look like who could demonstrate love, joy, peace, patience, kindness, goodness, faithfulness, gentleness, and self-control in each situation he or she encountered? Why, I think he would look just like...Christ. He would reveal Christ's nature to everyone around him. What greater fruit could there possibly be?

Fruitfulness has nothing to do with how many Bible

studies I've taught or how many people I've led to Christ, nor has it any attachment to any other religious activity. *Fruit is borne in our character.* It is the transformation of our lives so that we reflect God's nature to the culture around us. In John 15 the call to fruitfulness and the command to love one another are one and the same.

When we love the way God loves, we bear the fruit of his kingdom. It's what he wants to work into us through the long process of growth and maturity. The fruits of the Spirit are not what we can make ourselves do for a moment, but what God makes us to be for a lifetime. At its fulfillment this fruit is how we freely respond to people and situations. Obviously, this kind of fruit is not produced overnight. Learning to respond like Christ is fashioned in us over time as God walks us through our joys and disappointments, all the while transforming us from the very depths of our being.

The fruits of the Spirit are not what we can make ourselves do for a moment, but what God makes us to be for a lifetime.

Our ability to reveal God's image to the people around us is more important than our worship, our prayers, our religious deeds, our devotions, our spiritual gifts, even our acts of evangelism. For without this fruitfulness there is no spiritual work that counts, no evangelism that succeeds, and no gift that prevails. All of these other aspects are valuable in our growth in God's kingdom, but these are not the fruit that God seeks in our lives. If the objective of our time in worship or Bible study is not to allow God to transform us into his image with ever-increasing glory, then it means nothing!

Who hasn't seen people who have done great things for God, or been used in tremendous ways by the Lord, but whose lack of love, gentleness, or self-control rears its ugly head to mar all else that has been accomplished.

First Corinthians 13 is right: Without love we're just a loud crashing sound, regardless of whatever other successes we might be able to point to.

How is the world to know we are his disciples? Is it by our ornate church edifices? Is it by the breadth of our TV or radio ministries? Is it by the expensive musical productions or complicated children's programs? Is it through our sharp advertisements or minutely-planned worship services?

No! None of these are wrong in themselves, but we've got to recognize that what the world waits to see is a people who demonstrate God's character by the way they treat one another, by whether or not they are laying down their lives for one another in the same way Jesus did for them. They watch to see if we're serving each other, giving up our comfort for one another, forgiving each other—in short, loving each other deeply. If not, why should they believe? The only image of God the world will see is what he stamps on our lives.

**What the world waits to see is a people
who demonstrate God's character
by the way they treat one another,
by whether or not they are laying down
their lives for one another
in the same way Jesus did for them.**

Jesus said so—right in the midst of all his instructions about the vineyard: "This is to my Father's glory, that you bear much fruit, showing yourselves to be my disciples" (John 15:8). Notice that Jesus didn't spend much time teaching his disciples to plan crusades or door-to-door campaigns. He had already told them earlier that evening what the fruit was what both the Father and the world were looking for: "By this all men will know that you are my disciples, if you love one another" (John 13:35).

This is Jesus' model for evangelism. For all our technical expertise, we are sorely lacking in our ability to demonstrate to the world a self-sacrificing community where there is love and honor instead of backbiting, manipulating, and complaining.

They witness church split after church split. Consider this: In December of 1989 our congregation helped plant a new congregation in a village in central Mexico that had no church of any kind. When some of our team returned to Mexico three months later they found two churches, split apart by a dispute about eternal security—both believing that members of the other congregation were no longer Christians.

Our first thoughts were, Where did they learn such nonsense? They hadn't known salvation long enough to even contemplate such matters. Then we learned that outside people had come in to exploit what God was doing for their own gain.

No wonder the world rejects the gospel we preach! Why shouldn't it? If love does not fill the house of God, how will people know that he is real? Without intimate love overflowing his church we are only a loud noise that the world will never comprehend. The quality of our lives is the only platform on which we can ever stand as far as the world is concerned. What we say of God's nature is far less important than what we demonstrate.

Without intimate love overflowing his church we are only a loud noise that the world will never comprehend.

Each time we lay down our lives for another person we allow this world to see what happened 2,000 years ago at Calvary. Our sacrifices make the cross and God's love visible to people around us.

This is the fruit of the vineyard. All the Father's efforts toward us are to see his character filling our lives and spilling out from them like grape bunches on an over-loaded vine. As it is his passion, so it can be ours.

7

WHAT OF UNPRODUCTIVE VINES?

If anyone does not remain in me, he is
like a branch that is thrown away and withers;
such branches are picked up, thrown
into the fire and burned.
JOHN 15:6

Fruitless branches are obvious. The branch itself may look fine, but the canes that spring from it are withered and sickly. Few if any of them will even reach up to the wire intended to support them.

I've seen it happen a thousand times and each time it seems such a waste. It takes many years for a branch to develop, and each branch holds the potential for bearing much fruit. But when it was obvious that a branch was no longer capable of bearing fruit, I had to cut it off.

I'd fall to my knees beside the vine and pull the pruning saw from my back pocket. Unfolding the blade I would saw off the fruitless branch, tossing the dead wood into the middle of the row. Because branches were too big to be churned into the soil as canes are, they would be collected later.

So it is in God's vineyard. He is so passionate about fruitfulness that the consequences of not bearing fruit are dire indeed. Jesus didn't want that warning to escape us. After describing himself as the vine and the Father as the gardener he drives home this point. The Father cuts off every branch that doesn't bear fruit.

He goes on to describe five other things that happen to that branch. It is thrown away, cast off as worthless. Lying alone it withers to a hardened mass of dead wood. The only thing left to do is to gather them up and throw them into the fire to be burned.

Of all the things that happen to the branch the only one that ultimately matters is the first. Once a branch is cut off its life ends. What happens after that only describes what is left to be done with a dead branch. Without the life-giving connection to the rest of the vine, the sap dries out. What else can you do with that branch now but burn it?

When Ezekiel confronted Israel with her continuing rebellion against God, he reminded the people of just that fact. Did they really have any other purpose than to please God?

> *Son of man, how is the wood of a vine better than that of a branch on any of the trees in the forest? Is wood ever taken from it to make anything useful? Do they make pegs from it to hang things on?*
> EZEKIEL 15:2,3

Certainly not! Grapevines are not all-purpose plants; they are good only for producing grapes. If the vine doesn't do that its wood isn't useful for anything else. You can't eat it, build with it, or make tools of it.

Some people in our section of the country do use grape canes for craft projects. They twist the canes together to form a wreath and then decorate it with dried flowers, wooden geese, and billowy ribbons. Actually, I've never gotten used to these wreaths. No matter how you dress up dead branches, I've lived too long on a grape ranch to think of them as anything other than fire fuel or fertilizer for next year's crop.

The gardener prunes away those branches that do not bear fruit. His warning could be crudely stated as: "Bear fruit or burn." For that is what happens to fruitless branches. As we shall see in subsequent chapters, however, his point is not for them to go out and try to bear fruit, but for them to stay attached to the vine. Do that, he tells them and you can't help but bear fruit.

His point is not for them to go out and try to bear fruit, but for them to stay attached to the vine.

So in the next breath Jesus assured his disciples that the warning is not specifically directed at them. They were not in danger of being cut off since he had already made them clean. Jesus makes a play on words here. The word for clean is derived from the same root as the word for pruning earlier in the passage. Branches can be pruned up, or pruned off. The disciples had already been pruned up—cleansed by the word Jesus had spoken to them.

Jesus was not threatening them. He just wanted them to understand the Father's passion for fruitfulness, for it would help them understand the Father's work in them. God, it seems, has as little use for unfruitful branches as farmers do. No matter how lovely the branch might be, if it doesn't bear fruit it must be removed. The Father is not looking for lovely branches but ripening fruit.

Some of the stories from Jesus' life that have bothered me the most were of the times Jesus turned away seemingly promising candidates for the kingdom. A man wanted to follow him, but he needed to bury his father first. Jesus' response was harsh: "Let the dead bury their own dead, but you go and proclaim the kingdom of God" (Luke 9:60).

Or what of the time when the rich young ruler wanted to follow Jesus, but Jesus was only going to let him do so if he would sell everything he owned and give it to the poor? The young man left discouraged because he was not willing to do this.

Once Jesus even chased off a crowd of more than 5,000 who had eaten of the miraculous lunch of multiplied bread and fish, and then pursued Jesus around the Sea of Galilee. To these he said, "Eat my flesh and drink my blood." The crowd didn't understand his cryptic words and went away confused and disillusioned, wondering if he was inviting them to cannibalism. What bothers me is that Jesus didn't stop them. He didn't run after them and straighten out their misunderstanding, "Hey, come back! I was talking about communion."

These people seemed far more serious about pursuing the Lord than many I have seen today. Why did he eliminate these with challenges certainly more difficult than many new converts today would be able to bear?

Or was Jesus looking at something far deeper? Could he see that these were branches that were not going to plant deep enough to bear fruit? The first man would always cater to his family at the expense of the kingdom. The money of the young ruler would always be his real god, and trying to have both would only provide endless frustration. Was the crowd with satisfied bellies looking only for a free lunch, while lacking the faith that would endure the many other times when God's activity would defy their reason?

Perhaps Jesus realized that without some choice for change these people would not be fruitful and would need to be cut off anyway. There is an accountability to the kingdom that grace does not mask. Grace does not negate the effects of our failure to remain plugged into him as the vine. We cannot hide behind it as an excuse not to bear fruit. To make us fruitful is the very reason grace has been extended to us:

> *So, my brothers, you also died to the law through the body of Christ, that you might belong to another, to him who was raised from the dead, in order that we might bear fruit to God.*

> ROMANS 7:4

I am constantly amazed by those people who want the smallest bite of salvation they can take and still feel confident they can escape hell. The Father has opened to us a glorious kingdom where we can live in him and know the fullest of joy. Why settle for less?

But maybe you have. Maybe you've spent years near the kingdom of God, yet you do not see fruitfulness flowing from your life. Is there hope for you? Will the Father cut you off, or has he already?

Is there hope for you? Will the Father cut you off, or has he already?

Though God's judgment concerning our fruitlessness is certain, it is not always swift. Jesus tells another parable to illustrate his Father's heart for the vineyard that bears repeating. Though the vineyard that Jesus used in this parable is full of figs, the application of his teaching is no less vital to our understanding. Here we see that though the Father yearns for fruitfulness, his patience far exceeds that of any farmer I know.

> *A man had a fig tree, planted in his vineyard, and he went to look for fruit on it, but did not find any. So he said to the man who took care of the vineyard, "For three years now I've been coming to look for fruit on this fig tree and haven't found any. Cut it down! Why should it use up the soil?"*

*"Sir," the man replied, "leave it alone for one more
year, and I'll dig around it and fertilize it. If it bears
fruit next year, fine! If not, then cut it down."*

LUKE 13:6-9

In this brief parable the farmer comes to the vineyard
disappointed at the fruitlessness of one of the vines. He
had planted it three years ago, but it had not yet borne
any fruit. No farmer would expect a vine to be in full
production in three years, but it is extremely unusual for
a vine to grow that long without any fruit appearing.

He is ready to cut it down and replace it with a new
vine that will bear fruit, but the gardener here has a better hope: Let's give it another chance; I'll do everything
I can to encourage its fruitfulness, and then if it still
doesn't bear fruit we'll cut it down.

Jesus tells the parable to let the caretaker's heart reveal
the Father's. Here again he differs from the farmer who
only looks at the bottom line. Yes, the track record may
not be good, but we still have three years' worth of roots
here. Let's try one more year, doing all we can to coax
fruitfulness out of the vine.

Behold the immense patience of our God! He sees
potential where we often miss it and is willing to invest
all his resources in one more attempt at fruitfulness.
Cutting off the unfruitful is never God's first choice; it is
only his last resort.

God still has hope for fruitfulness from your life even
if it feels as though you've squandered the preceding
years. If you are still hungry and willing to respond to
the Father, your time is not up yet.

Those who hunger after the Father will want to bear
fruit. It is not a difficult path for he does not ask us to
produce it. Only Jesus can make us fruitful as he lives his
life through us. The point of this passage is staying
plugged into the vine. Do that and you'll have more
fruit than you know what to do with.

8

WON'T YOU BE MY FRIEND?

Greater love has no one than this,
that he lay down his life for his friends.
You are my friends if you do what I command.
JOHN 15:13,14

"I am the vine; you are the branches." Almost poetic in
its simplicity, Jesus comes to the crowning theme of his
lesson. For one who has grown up around grapevines, it
is a jarring statement.

Few plants come in as many fascinating shapes as
grapevines. Their trunks twist up from the ground in a
myriad of shapes and forms. Two feet or so above the
ground the trunk separates into craggy arms that continue the seemingly random twisting and turning as
they reach toward the wires above. One of the games we
played as children was to challenge each other to imper-
sonate a chosen grapevine by contorting our own trunk
and limbs to match it.

Thinking back, I can't ever remember making much of
a distinction between the vine and the branches. The
same rough, flaky bark that starts just above the ground

continues out through the branches where the canes emerge. I think of a vine as one unit made up of both trunk and branches. The disciples, who had seen thousands of vines, would have thought similarly.

If you asked me to go out today and saw off a branch for you, I could do it easily enough. But in looking at a grapevine up close there is nothing about the makeup of a branch that distinguishes it from a trunk. There is no fixed line that says the vine ends here and the branch begins. I could saw from the point at which it separates from another branch, but the cut line would only be arbitrary. You would not know when I was done if I had all branch, or sawed part of the vine in the process.

When Jesus called himself the vine and us the branches, he could have chosen no better illustration of the intimate bond he seeks with his followers. He desires that we identify so closely with him that others cannot tell where he leaves off and where we begin. We become so one with him, that his life is reflected through us.

He desires that we identify so closely with him that others cannot tell where he leaves off and where we begin.

No branch has any life in itself, only the vine does. A branch can only have life when it draws it from another source. It needs to be connected. Could there be a better picture of our need for Jesus' life in us or a better explanation of why we are so empty without him?

The Father created us to receive life, not produce it. We are by act of creation empty vessels. To have life, we need to draw life from something. That explains why we often feel empty and why we look for life in so many other places and by doing so carry so many disappointed expectations. Who has not sought out a new job, home or other possession, certain that it would fulfill their deepest desire, only to find that the joy it provided quickly faded away? How many of our relationships are so loaded with expectations of what that person should provide for us that we're constantly disappointed in them when they fall short? People seek out alcohol and drugs with the same hopes, and in the end the same disappointments.

Jesus made clear at the outset of this parable that he was not just a vine, but the *true* vine. This was exclusive terminology. His phrasing assumes there are other 'vines' in our world that promise fulfillment and fruitfulness, but cannot provide it. He is the only true one. All others are imposters.

We should know that well, for we have all plugged into things that promised fullness when they really only stole it from us. The greatest moments of joy in this world quickly fade away, leaving us more empty than we were before.

This picture takes us to the heart of God's purpose in his desire to save us. Salvation was not merely our reprieve from hell, but a doorway through which we could enter into the fullness of his life. Those who regard salvation only as an escape from eternal punishment develop a maintenance mentality about their lives. They hold on to God just enough to ensure that they don't lose their salvation

But Jesus invited his followers to so much more. He wanted us to plunge our lives so deeply into his, that our life would be swallowed up by his. He did not offer hollow promises of life, but life itself. By drawing that life we would bear the fruit of his Father's character. This is no mere maintenance mentality; he invited us on an adventure into the depths of God that the ancients could only dream about and in which we will never be disappointed.

For Jesus went on to define the exact nature of the incredible link that joins a branch to the vine: "I have called you friends." How do we become branches on the vine and draw his life? We accept his marvelous offer of a personal friendship with him and the Father.

How do we become branches on his vine and draw his life? We accept his marvelous offer of a personal friendship with him and the Father.

Few things are more marvelous than a good friendship. What a joy whenever we find someone who reciprocates our pleasure at being with him or her, respects our ideas, gets involved in our struggles and successes and offers us the safety of always being honest and genuine. Good friendships are filled with tenderness, spontaneity and warmth.

Take everything that you know about a good friendship, picking the best you've ever experienced, and you'll understand the wonder of Jesus' invitation to you. He wants to be the best friend you ever had—sharing every moment of your life. And, unlike any other friend you've ever had, this one will never fail you.

One winter afternoon not so long ago I blazed up the field following the kickoff, maneuvering myself to get a sure tackle on the receiver. As he approached he made a move toward the sideline. I turned toward him to shove him out-of-bounds when suddenly he cut back to the left. I tried to cut with him, but my feet slipped out from under me on the wet grass. I reached out to grab him in one last desperate attempt, but went sliding by hopelessly as he cut up the middle and scored a touchdown.

My ten-year-old came trotting back up the field laughing so hard that he crumpled on the ground next to me. "You should have seen your face!" Andy cackled.

I laughed with him there on the grass. We had been playing for half an hour, and I was exhausted. We talked about some of the best plays and laughed together. All the while we were being constantly pestered by our yellow Labrador, who kept dropping a tennis ball on various parts of our anatomy, hoping we would hurl it across the lawn for her to chase. Catching my wind, I devised a plan. "I'll throw her tennis ball toward the end of the lawn, then let's both go after her like she's returning a kickoff." Andy was excited at the prospect.

I tossed the ball and off went the dog in full stride. We jumped to our feet and pursued her. She never knew we were coming until she picked up the tennis ball, wheeled around, and saw the two of us running at her screaming. The shocked look on her face was worth the whole exercise as she bolted around us, unable to figure out what we were doing. Again we collapsed to the ground laughing at the dog and each other. As our laughter slowly drained we lingered awhile, talking of Andy's day at school, news he had heard on the TV that evening, and a variety of other things.

Of such moments intimacy is created. I am responsible to train Andy in the ways of God, but I do that best only to the degree that I am his friend. My friendship with him does not demean my fatherhood, but defines it. This friendship allows me the difficult moments of demanding his obedience without compromising our relationship or his self-respect.

In no less a way does Jesus invite us to friendship with him. He wants us to know him with the same kind of warmth, to laugh with him through our slips and spills. He wants to relax with us in our weariness, to commune with us on the issues that affect us most. Though most believers are comfortable speaking of a "personal relationship with Jesus," few concepts are so greatly celebrated and so-little experienced.

Though most believers are comfortable speaking of a "personal relationship with Jesus," few concepts are so greatly celebrated and so little experienced.

Some people shy away from intimacy with Jesus, preferring instead to concentrate on his transcendence: He is the great Lord who by a word spoke worlds into existence. They have seen the imbalance of people who feign a chumminess with Jesus that isn't quite real and often not respectful of his greatness. But that can be an excuse for a greater personal emptiness.

Often what lies beneath the theology of a distant God is frustration at God's seeming inactivity. Prayers go unanswered. Requests for wisdom seem caught in a backlog of celestial red tape. In our darkest moments he did not come and change our circumstances. To allay disappointment we may prefer the simplistic explanation that friendship with God is an abstract thing, and then find some measure of comfort in resignation that his ways are higher than ours.

But God's awesomeness and his nearness are not conflicting images. His nearness only makes his greatness that much more awesome. What so-called god in any other religion or legend has ever displayed such greatness of power and such warm tenderness toward people? Who else has subjected himself to the sin of his own creation by suffering such unjustified punishment against himself for its salvation?

Such intimacy does not diminish his lordship, but brings it to our lives in the most powerful way possible: In the tenderness of a warm friendship. That tenderness is no better demonstrated than the way Jesus loved his worried followers the night before he was crucified.

Such intimacy does not diminish his lordship, but brings it to our lives in the most powerful way possible.

They begged him for alternatives to his impending departure. Surely you won't leave us. We'll stay with you no matter what. Can't we go with you?

He was not deaf to their cries, but little did they realize that if he fulfilled their limited expectations it would deny them the greater joy he had in store for them. So he sat down and ate with them, took them for a walk in a garden, and taught them how to pray in moments of conflict in a way that invites God closer and does not push him away.

Jesus was being their friend *through* the circumstances he wouldn't change. He promised them another Counselor who would be with them forever. He makes clear his invitation: I want to be your friend. Will you be mine?

The offer of friendship is the crowning point of his tale of the vine. Jesus offered his disciples fullness of joy and challenged them to be fruitful for the Father, but neither of these were to be the object of their pursuit. Seek fulfillment and you will only find hollow days of temporal satisfaction that fade as fast as a snowflake on a warm car. Try to make yourself fruitful and you'll only know the endless frustration of good deeds that never fulfill their intentions, and effort that never seems enough to satisfy God.

The fulfillment and fruitfulness Jesus offered is only found in our friendship with him. That's what he told us to seek. How we develop that friendship and remain in it daily will occupy the chapters ahead. It is the essence of life in God's vineyard, defining how we as branches are joined to the true vine.

Don't ever let your relationship with Jesus become overgrown with anything other than the simplicity of friendship. He wants you to enjoy him. Marriages begin to fail the day husbands and wives become so concerned about the work of survival that they forget how to enjoy each other. So does our relationship with God. We can be so absorbed in any activity—especially religious activity— and forget to enjoy his friendship.

Nothing could be more tragic, for he wants to go with you everywhere—not only to church and ministry outreaches but also to a camping trip with your family, a round of golf with friends, and even a backyard football game with your children.

9

I'VE BEEN CHOSEN

You did not choose me, but I chose you.
JOHN 15:16

What gives any of us the right to presume such intimacy with one so magnificent? The answer is found in how we came to be a branch on the Lord's vine to begin with.

At first glance over Jesus' words about the vineyard it is easy to miss. He didn't describe it in detail, since those he talked to were already firmly implanted in the vine, but he did remind them how it all began.

"I chose you." It was that simple. They had not come to him by their own determination or because they just happened to be at the right place at the right time. Their participation in his life was not a random act of nature. He had chosen them.

I wonder how much those words meant to Peter on this treacherous night. Circumstances were tumbling downhill with increasing velocity. Danger and confusion swirled in the darkness. He must have thought, How did I get myself into this?

"I chose you." The words must have leapt out at him. I remember now; that's exactly the way it happened. How vividly that day would have remained in Peter's memory: Exhausted from a long and unsuccessful night at sea, he had just finished cleaning the nets when Jesus approached him. What Peter knew about Jesus before that moment is unclear. We do know that even after his discouraging night of fishing, he consented to Jesus' request to use his boat to speak to the crowd.

Evidently impressed to some degree, Peter calls Jesus "Master" shortly after he is finished, and even agrees to another odd request from Jesus. Yes, he'll put out the nets again—even though they caught nothing the night before and were now lying at his feet perhaps already cleaned and folded for another night's work.

He had hardly slipped them overboard when the water began to boil with fish leaping into his net. The load was too big for one man, and he called for help. Though Peter's eyes may have been on the net, his heart was fixed on this incredible man. "Go away from me, Lord; I am a sinful man."

Jesus didn't honor Peter's request, but instead invited him to go fishing with him; this time for people. That was all it took. Peter left the greatest catch of his life for others to sell.

I've met two kinds of people who are disappointed by the lack of reality they have found in their relationship with the Savior. The first I have described in previous chapters—those who blame God for not caring enough to help them. Peter is an example of the other type— those who feel like damaged goods. They are too filthy, too ugly to tolerate God's presence. They will tell him to leave them alone, and if he doesn't they'll run away themselves.

But Peter had been chosen, and by that simple act his fears were dispelled. Here is an amazing attribute of this vine, unlike any I've ever seen: Jesus chooses the branches that will draw life from him. This was not Peter's doing. He had not earned it.

Here is an amazing attribute of this vine, unlike any I've ever seen: Jesus chooses the branches that will draw life from him.

What a difference from anything else in his culture. "If you want something, go out and get it. No one is going to walk up and hand it over to you." This was especially true of religion. The religious leaders were a select class; they had to have money or connections to surface at the top of the ladder. But in one moment on a makeshift dock Jesus short-circuits the process. Reaching past those who had completed the religious obstacle course of the day he simply chooses Peter. "I want you; will you come?"

Jesus makes the same invitation to us, because branches in his vineyard don't just grow naturally out of his vine, like they did in my father's field. Jesus' words harken back to a far more special process called grafting.

The most detailed picture of how grafting works is painted by Paul in Romans 11:17-24. Though he writes of olive trees, the same process was also used in vineyards. And though he writes in generalities of the Jewish and Gentile nations, he illustrates what we all go through on a personal level so that we can become partakers of God's life.

Grafting is a nearly-miraculous process in which one new plant is made out of two different ones. There are various methods for doing this, but all involve a branch cut from one vine and inserted into a cut on another vine. The two are then bound together with an adhesive compound or tape (or in ancient days mud or clay). As the wound heals, the two plants become one, the new branch drawing sap from the roots of the established vine.

Notice that grafting demands a wound in both parties. Jesus, as our vine, was cut open on the cross to make room for us. For us to be grafted into him we must also be wounded in complementary fashion so that we will fit into the place prepared. That's why we have to identify with the death of Christ and die to whatever we were before coming to him. Unless we are cut away from our roots in the past we cannot be placed in him.

As Israel was "broken off because of unbelief," the only way we can be grafted in is by believing in him. Believing in Jesus means that we will surrender our life to his control and trust his word about everything.

This reaches to the very heart of Paul's analogy. He points out that grafting is "contrary to nature" and as such superbly illustrates our new Christian life. We can no longer trust the natural ways of our flesh since we've become part of something so wonderfully new.

Usually cultivated branches were grafted onto wild roots, which were more vigorous, but Paul turns the analogy here. We are the wild shoots because of the hostile and ignorant ways of our flesh. Jesus is the cultivated vine. If we are going to experience God's life we're going to have to draw from his roots.

The reason this is so important for us to know who chose whom at the outset is not only because of the confidence it gives us to pursue Jesus with hope and joy, but because it sets a serious precedent for everything about the Father's vineyard.

He is my total resource for strength, nourishment, comfort, and direction. Everything to the branch flows through the trunk. Moisture and nutrients from the soil are delivered to the branches on the vine's timetable. As that vine, Jesus sets the direction for my life. He chooses my portion today, my ministry, my feeding. I am to become totally dependent upon him, a responder in the life of the kingdom, not an initiator. Nothing happens by my choice unless it was first his.

I am to become totally dependent upon him, a responder in the life of the kingdom, not an initiator.

Grafting is a process that can only be done one branch at a time. It requires the personal attention of the gardener as he cuts and fits us into Christ, and a personal response from us. Each of us must respond to his work, because God has no second-generation disciples.

My wife and I are getting to watch that process right now in our 12-year-old daughter. Sara and I are actively helping Julie develop her own relationship with God and find an accountability to him that does not run through her parents. We began on her twelfth birthday to release an increasing number of decisions into Julie's hand so that we can help her through the sometimes painful process of learning to hear and believe God's voice.

And it's paying off. Recently she was invited to a birthday party of a good friend. This was to be a sleepover event, and since this friend lives out of town, Julie would be the only one not from her friend's school. The last few years when she has attended daytime parties for this girl, she has felt left out because all the other girls were such good friends.

"Do I have to go, Dad?" she asked with a disgusted whine. She knew from plenty of past times that we made them go to the parties of children whom they have invited to their own.

"Julie, you're 12 now and the decision is yours. I'm not going to make you go. You need to decide for yourself what is right to do."

Immediately her countenance changed. "Should I go?" the whine was now gone. I wasn't going to make her go and by that simple act I had become someone who could now help her with the decision.

"She came to your last party."

"I know, but, Dad, everyone leaves me out." The whine had returned.

"I'm not saying you have to go. I'm only helping you see what to consider. Have you prayed about it yet?" This time I got a scrunched-up nose and that look of "whatever for?" "Why don't you go up to your room and ask God what he wants you to do? If he wants you to go, then go. If not, then don't."

She did exactly that, and 20 minutes later she came back out on the landing. "I'm going to go to the party," she said with a broad smile. It's so much harder to be accountable to God than it is to manipulate a parent, but so much more joyful.

It was a small matter, but my relationship to my daughter is changing. God now needs the place I have had in her life for her first years. Julie has a heart for God and a desire to please him, and I need to release her to be grafted into that vine as well. Though I risk letting her make mistakes, I would much rather have her make them in small things like birthday parties when I'm close enough to walk her through them than when she's choosing a mate for life a thousand miles away.

Without being personally grafted in, our life in God will always be empty and irrelevant. We cannot afford to let a parent, pastor, or Bible study leader be grafted in for us. We dare not try to draw our life from them—only from Jesus himself.

**Without being personally grafted in,
our life in God will always be
empty and irrelevant.**

What about you? Jesus not only chose those first disciples, he continues to choose his followers today. *He* is the one who guarantees our place alongside him. He wants *us*, not our abilities or talents. Whatever excuses we think might prevent that grafting must dissolve along with Peter's, because it was Jesus' choice before it was ever ours.

Anyone who has ever waited in line, only to be the last chosen for a team, knows the terrifying humiliation of not being wanted. Regrettably, many of us carry that same feeling into Christianity. "Whosoever will" has come to mean that God *has* to take everybody. So when God says, "You are a chosen people, a royal priesthood, a holy nation, a people belonging to God..." it doesn't mean anything to us. Yet there is no greater assurance than knowing that Jesus has chosen us to be planted in him.

There is no greater assurance than knowing that Jesus has chosen us to be planted in him.

What is especially magnificent about the Lord's choosing is that *his choosing me does not exclude anyone else.* When five people compete for a new position in the company, the joy of the person selected is purchased at the severe disappointment of the other four. In the Father's vineyard, however, there is a time (even numerous times) in every life when God extends his hand to choose each person. Not all walk over to join his team, however. Many walk away unwilling to give up their life to gain his.

But why do I pursue abiding in the vine with such fervor? Because no matter how unloved I've felt in the past, no matter how filthy I feel in my sin, God knew all of that when he chose me to be on his team. He wanted *me*, and he also wants *you*. Hope for finding fulfillment in his kingdom springs from that simple truth. You can have fulfillment in his kingdom specifically because *he wants to give it to you.*

I don't know if this was a source of comfort to Peter the morning after he denied Jesus. If it had been me, I'd have come back to Jesus' simple words the night before. Jesus knew well how weak Peter's flesh would be in this trial. Yet to him and the others he still said, "I have chosen you."

When it comes down to our relationship with Jesus, what else really matters?

10

IF...

If a man remains in me
and I in him, he will bear much fruit;
apart from me you can do nothing.
JOHN 15:5

In the vineyards of this world, branches don't have freedom of choice. They are silent victims of whatever the farmer or his workers decide to be their lot.

Each winter as I pruned vines in my father's vineyard, I had total freedom to shape the vine any way I chose. It was my decision which branches should remain and which would be cut off. I was master of that vine, and I chose at times almost on a whim which branches might be robust enough to promise a good harvest ahead.

The branches had nothing to say about it, no volition of their own. Branches are unthinking objects. They had no ability to prune themselves even if they wanted to, or stick themselves back on the vine after I had cut them off. They were victims pure and simple, without any voice or choice in the matter.

But here the Father's vineyard takes another major

departure from our earthly ones, for in his vineyard the branches have their own will. No one compels them to grow here. The Father has set the stage, but it is their choice whether or not they want to be part of the drama of life in the vineyard.

The Father has set the stage, but it is their choice whether or not they want to be part of the drama of life in the vineyard.

Jesus conveyed that truth to his own followers with a simple two-letter word: "if." Five times in these short 16 verses Jesus uses if. Each time it is followed by a simple statement highlighting the role that the branch plays in being part of this vineyard.

- *If* a man remains in me and I in him, he will bear much fruit.
- *If* anyone does not remain in me, he is like a branch that is thrown away and withers.
- *If* you remain in me and my words remain in you, ask whatever you wish, and it will be given you.
- *If* you obey my commands, you will remain in my love.
- You are my friends *if* you do what I command.

If. A simple word to state simple realities. Do this and that will happen. Don't do it and something else will. Cause and effect, quick and clean. The apostle John, perhaps better than anyone else, picked up the stark contrast of this simple word. He uses "if" 74 times in his gospel and 21 times in his first brief epistle.

"If" allows no room for maybes, as if Jesus' words were mere wishful thinking or statements of probability. These are simple facts, simply stated, without loopholes or mitigating circumstances. This is the way God has set things up. Choose to come along, or choose not to. The decision is ours.

There is no better way to define the balance between God's sovereignty and our free will. For our free will does not mean, cannot mean, that the branches have the run of the vineyard. This is *the Father's* vineyard. He made it and he determined how it will function. We are free to choose whether or not we want to be part of it, but we cannot change the way God's vineyard functions in order to please ourselves.

If we do not choose to remain in the vine and be fruitful, we cannot also choose to hang around the vineyard anyway; he will cut us away. Certainly many people want God's favor and blessing on their lives. Who would say no to that? But even with that desire, many persist in living life by their own wisdom, following the appetites of their own flesh.

Somehow, they hope, grace will extend beyond their own selfishness and failure to submit to God's ways. I'm not talking here about those who war against their flesh as they fall victim to it, but those who willingly give in to their appetites hoping that God will somehow override the consequences of their choices.

While growing up I always wanted the money that Dad paid us for working in the vineyard, but I never wanted to do the work to get it. What a dilemma! I wanted to play all the time, but still have the rewards of those who worked. I face the same attitude in my children today. They like being the beneficiaries of the work that needs to be done around the house—clean clothes and dishes—but they struggle with being participants in the process of gaining them.

For a branch in God's vineyard this simply cannot be. The "if" clauses of this passage compel us to make a choice. That choice is not whether we want to be fulfilled in God's life, or whether we want to be fruitful for his kingdom. The choice is whether or not we will accept his offer of friendship by remaining in him.

If we do, an array of dazzling opportunities are offered

to each of us. If not, we are confronted with certain judgment. The branch dries up and is thrown away. Why? Because one powerful reality lies behind all of Jesus' teaching on the vineyard: "Apart from me you can do nothing." When we cut ourselves off from relationship with Jesus, we are incapable of doing anything in God's kingdom. This doesn't mean we won't be busy in any number of religious activities on his behalf, but simply that none of these will bear the fruit of his kingdom.

One powerful reality lies behind all of Jesus' teaching on the vineyard: "Apart from me you can do nothing."

How I wish this were as clear in the spiritual vineyard as it is in the earthly one! The moment a branch cuts itself off from the life-giving nourishment of the vine it begins to wither. Almost immediately the leaves begin to sag, and though they're still green, their limpness tells you that death has already come.

With us, however, we can become distracted from Jesus' involvement in our lives and hardly even notice it. We can still be engrossed in a wide variety of spiritual activities. His blessing still seems to accompany us even as we get by on our own strength, unaware of the creeping death that has been unleashed. Then one day we wake up feeling empty or stressed by the demands on our lives. We wonder why God doesn't seem as close to us as before, never recognizing that we have drawn back from the vine.

Simple neglect of our friendship with Jesus is the biggest danger any of us will face. It happens so easily, because like vines we are easily distracted from his presence by the challenges and opportunities of our culture.

Vines are crafty plants, always looking for nourishment wherever they can find it. They are notorious for rooting wherever they are given the chance. All a cane has to do is fall to the ground and if the dirt covers it the same buds that are meant to produce fruit and leaves are just as happy to produce roots instead. These roots can become so strong that they draw their own nourishment from the soil and if cut off from the vine these branches will become their own vine. It happens so simply that it is one of the chief ways vines are propagated on earth, but not in the Father's kingdom!

Listen to Jeremiah's lament: "I had planted you like a choice vine of sound and reliable stock. How then did you turn against me into a corrupt, wild vine?" (Jeremiah 2:21). How indeed! It happens when branches themselves sink roots into the ground to develop their own roots and seek their own nourishment. Branches are not supposed to have roots—just canes, leaves, and fruit.

What a picture of our own lives! That's why without even noticing it we seek out the false vines we discussed in the last chapter. Even while we seek to follow Jesus, the enemy lures us with opportunities to sink our roots into the simplest things.

About every six months one family in our congregation banishes their television set to the garage for a few weeks. They don't do that because they consider it evil, but because they recognize at times how much it dominates their attention. At some point it crosses the line from being a tool they can use for information and entertainment and instead becomes a resource for coping with boredom and a distraction to their relationship with the Father. It begins to control them, and they are sensitive enough when that happens to cut it off before their roots sink into it.

Many people struggle with other things. Eating is a natural and delightful gift of God, but the enemy has tempted many people to sink their roots into it as a way to deal with pain and misery. Other people deal with their anxieties by shopping, abusing drugs or alcohol, or overdosing on their chosen form of recreation. When our roots sink into these as a means to live our lives, our life in Christ will whither.

Why do we do it? Because there are so many things that can at least temporarily make us feel good. They do provide temporary relief, and often far more easily than we can find it in the cross of Christ. But these things only *cover* pain, they don't actually heal it. In time the pain returns in ever-haunting ways, demanding even more degrading attempts to mask it.

The result of rooting in anything but Jesus is bondage and destruction. Promising instant gratification, the devices of this world offer no true healing. Apart from him we will not find any joy or fruit. In him, however, is life full and abundant.

In the next few chapters we will cover the implications of each of these "if" statements as we look at the qualities of friendship Jesus used to teach us how to remain in him and be a thriving branch on the vine. The way of the vine calls us not just to understand or even agree with Jesus' instructions, but to follow them.

The way of the vine calls us not just to understand or even agree with Jesus' instructions, but to follow them.

In recent decades of Christianity our approach to God's life has been mostly centered on creeds and confessions—the words of our mouth. Do you want to know Jesus? Pray this sinner's prayer with me. We ask people to confess to God what they want of him, without putting enough focus on the lifestyle we must embrace.

When we wander away from the faith disillusioned that God's promises didn't meet our expectations we need to be honest enough to probe whether or not our walk fulfilled the promises we made to him. In God's kingdom it matters less what we tell him we want to do than what we actually do.

Walter Wangerin in his book on marriage, *As for Me and My House,* illustrates this problem. A couple is planning to have a baby, and the husband promises that when they have it, he will cut back at work and help out more around the house. When the baby comes, however, he has been promoted, or has forgotten the intensity of his feelings, or has now realized that the home is less pleasant to be around than he imagined. Listen to his conclusion:

> *There are people who, to escape the burden of today, make wondrous promises against tomorrow. These people live in their words alone; they are infants in responsibility. More than their bond they think their words themselves are deeds! In fact, they are pleased to believe that by promising something they have already accomplished something.*

Too many of us make the promises and never get around to fulfilling them. No wonder our relationship remains lifeless and empty, because the quality of our friendship to Jesus hinges upon our active choice to remain in him.

That's what he has asked of us. Don't mistake responsive actions for outward efforts to earn God's grace through legalistic efforts. The responses given in this passage are first demonstrated in the heart and then reflected in actions. Jesus did not ask for perfection in our conduct, observance of religious rituals or laws, or sacrifices to demonstrate our sincerity—only for hearts that will stay in his presence no matter what!

11

STAY!

If a man remains in me and I in him,
he will bear much fruit.
JOHN 15:5

My prayer closet these days is a cotton field and plum orchard behind our home. I don't own them, but borrow them for a few moments most mornings. My dog is my faithful companion to these prayer times. She loves dashing through the fields hoping for a rabbit to chase or a pheasant to flush.

But having her that far out without a leash makes for some interesting moments, especially when we meet other dogs. Buffy has walked these fields ever since she was a puppy and assumes, I think, that they all belong to me. She will chase after anything that comes near, from Dobermans to horses. She even chased off a wild coyote that had taken up residence here.

Her only protection against the dangers of other animals and the roadways we walk near is her ability to understand one simple command: Stay!

Buffy knows it well enough, but I'll have to admit that whether or not she obeys it depends on how close she is to me when I call it. If she's too far away and the temptation is too great, lured by an aggressive dog intruding on "her" territory, she's off, and no amount of yelling will bring her back until the chase is spent. Then she returns with great remorse in her eyes. Even a dog knows it is easier to ask for forgiveness than permission!

So far she's always returned, because the object of her pursuit has always fled at her approach. I regret the day she meets an animal that stands its ground. I'll call her back, but it will work only if she will listen. If she'll just stay with me, I can keep her safe.

That same response is all Jesus asks of the branches in his vineyard. "Remain," he repeats throughout his lesson ten times to be exact, most of the time in the simple call to remain *in him*. His command should not be difficult to understand. It's the same as commanding a dog to stay, or giving instructions to your child as you plunge together into the midday crowd at the local mall. It's what I've said a thousand times to my children when they were younger as we set up our campsites in the mountains. "Stay nearby. If you wander so far that you can't see our camp, you've gone too far."

What Jesus intends here is just that simple, though admittedly far more powerful. On two fronts my analogy is too weak to convey the depth of our opportunity. First of all, when I call my dog to stay, or encourage it of my children, I mean it only for the moment when the situation is tenuous. When Jesus invites us to remain, however, it is no temporary request.

His word speaks of a persistent remaining, as in taking up residence. That's why some translations prefer the word "abide." This perhaps more aptly conveys the permanence of our relationship with Jesus. We don't just hang around his presence when trouble strikes, but we are called to remain in him all the time.

Unlike a wild animal that will only drink when it is

thirsty, the branch drinks from the vine all day every day. It never goes out on its own and never gets thirsty and comes back for a drink. It is there all the time. We cannot compartmentalize our spiritual life, making time for God like we do our work or play. Life in Christ permeates everything we do.

The second difference lies in the construction Jesus uses as he invites us to remain *in* him. Though it sounds fine when we speak of vines, it is a bit jarring when we refer to people. We naturally think of remaining *with* someone, not *in* them. But the level of intimacy that a branch has with the vine is the standard by which Jesus measures our relationship with him. This is an intimate link. We are not just staying *with* him, standing nearby, watching what's going on; we are linked *to* him. Our identity and existence are bound up in the vine.

We are not just staying *with* him, standing nearby, watching what's going on; we are linked *to* him.

It's no wonder that the phrase "in Christ" became a popular definition of the Christian life in the epistles. The early church understood the depth of intimacy that Jesus invited them to discover. They weren't just born-again Christians, as if they had joined a new club. They were people 'in Christ' daily drawing his life and daily reflecting his glory.

"Remain." The same thing Jesus asks of us he offers to us as well. Two times in this very passage he tells us that *he* will remain *in us*. Not only will we *live in him*, but he will *live in us*.

Jesus compares the depth of our relationship with him to the fellowship he shared with the Father. "You will remain in my love, just as I... remain in his love." We can know Jesus in the same way he knew his Father. The same intimacy that brought strength, wisdom, and comfort is available to us. What a marvelous promise; what a fantastic relationship to pursue! Growing in it will be a lifetime adventure. All we have to do is stay in the vine where the Father planted us.

What a contrast to everything this world teaches us. If we want anything in this life we have to *achieve* it, vesting our energies to somehow gain the thing we desire. But this is not true in God's vineyard. We don't have to achieve anything. When God established us in Christ he gave us a gift of friendship, regenerating our hearts, making us sensitive to his presence and his voice. All we need to do now is continue to embrace that friendship and not run off at every distraction or be pulled away by every temptation.

Stay attached—in the vineyard it's the only assignment a branch has. If nothing is allowed to sever it from the vine, it will be all it needs to be. The same is true of our life in God. If we'll remain in the vine, fruitfulness and fulfillment will accompany us wherever we go. If we fail to do that, it matters little what else we do, for we will inevitably end up empty and frustrated.

Remaining in him is as simple as regularly being where he is. Jesus doesn't hide from his followers, but clearly tells us where to find him. He has invested his presence in some very simple things—in his Word, in prayer, in our surrender to him, in the lives of other believers, and in serving people who are in need. Staying in his presence is as simple as meeting him regularly in these places.

He has invested his presence in some very simple things—in his Word, in prayer, in our surrender to him, in the lives of other believers, and in serving people who are in need.

What transforms any of these things from religious routine to life-giving nourishment from the vine is our own heart of worship. It's Jesus we're looking for in all of these places, and worship is the key to sensitive hearts that will come to his presence.

"Enter his gates with thanksgiving and his courts with praise; give thanks to him and praise his name" (Psalm 100:4). Our access to his presence rises out of praise and thanksgiving. God is worthy, and by affirming that in my own heart I am drawn away from my critical and complaining nature that serves only to separate myself from him. The Scriptures encourage us to cultivate moments throughout our days where we pause, if sometimes only for a few moments, to heighten our awareness of Jesus' presence with us by being thankful.

We remain in the vine by centering our whole lives on his presence in us. That begins in these special and intimate moments of friendship where we withdraw from the frenetic demands of our culture and steal away to our prayer closet, wherever and whatever that may be.

There we focus our attention on him, express our affection to him, and let him draw near to us. There he soothes our demanding fears, exposes our seductive flesh, or gives us his insights in the midst of our day. Sometimes his touch comes almost before we even turn our attention toward him, at others it comes after we have lingered, waiting on him and bringing our hearts to rest in his presence.

Having cultivated his presence in those moments, it is easy to invite his activity throughout the rest of our day in small snippets of time. I have often been in my office lost in the latest project demanding my attention only to be buzzed by my secretary and told that an appointment has arrived. I look at my watch in shock. Already! I'll push away from my desk, but before I go for my door, I'll bow my head before my Lord. My prayer at such times may be nothing more than, "Jesus, help me." But often, wonderfully often, in just such a moment he drops in my mind a nugget of wisdom into my heart that shapes my response toward that appointment.

That is how real Jesus wants your moments to be with

him. Being with him is not a religious duty, but a time for us to enjoy our friendship with him. He is faithful to those moments and by them transforms us ever more into his image, producing in us the fruit we so desire to offer him.

But remaining in him has a twofold meaning. Not only does it mean to stay in his presence by our daily responses to him, but it also stirs us to long-term faith-fulness, an attitude that will carry us through anything that comes our way.

12

FRIENDSHIP FOR
THE LONG HAUL

[I] appointed you to go and bear fruit—
fruit that will last.
JOHN 15:16

The only difference on a grapevine between a cane and a branch is longevity. A branch has been there for a long time. Its ability to transform the nourishment of the vine into a harvest of grapes results from its years of continued attachment to the vine.

Some of the branches in my father's vineyard are more than 40 years old, and yet they keep on yielding one harvest after another. Vineyards are long-term crops with mature vines producing far more than young ones.

As Jesus looked across those young men in the garden, he wanted them to know he wasn't inviting them to any short-term flash of brilliance. He had no desire to use them up, allowing their zealous lifestyles to burn out in a few short months or years. He challenged them to cultivate a relationship with him that would look to the long haul, that would still be there through the doubts

99

and fears this age would hurl at them.

He wanted fruitfulness from them that would last all of their lives. For the better fruit comes from the greater depth that the passing of time affords. He invited them to a friendship that time could not diminish, but make it only deeper and more glorious.

He invited them to a friendship that time could not diminish, but make it only deeper and more glorious.

Unfortunately our society knows so little of the beauty of long-term friendships. We are a transient culture, moving so frequently that lifelong friendships are indeed rare. Advertising preys on our penchant to become quickly bored with anything that becomes too familiar and lures us with the excitement of something new or different.

I sat across from a newlywed couple who had encountered their first seemingly insurmountable conflict. They were at an impasse and deeply concerned about the future of their relationship. "And the first year is supposed to be our best one," the wife said hopelessly.

No comment riles me more.

My wife and I have developed a friendship through three years of dating and 20 years of marriage. Sara and I have had that much practice loving each other and we are finally getting pretty good at it. We've let God shape us alongside each other so that we complement each other far more now than when we were first married.

We are now reaping the glorious benefits of long-term friendship: private jokes no one else can understand, thinking the same thing at almost the same moment, saying more to each other with a glance and a wink across a crowded room than less-practiced couples can say in a night of conversation. We laugh harder than we've ever laughed and hold each other more tenderly through difficult moments than we ever could a few years before. I can't wait to find out what this love affair will be like another 20 years from now.

The first year of marriage was never meant to be anyone's best. In our first year we were rookies, and though it was fun, every year since has become even better.

Jesus wants the same for us. Every year is meant to be better than the one before, because we've grown to know him better and have been changed more into his likeness. We've tasted of his faithfulness in the heat of battle and found it far more real than we ever dreamed.

Only long-termers discover that depth, those who've not allowed their trust to be compromised by the challenges in their life. You'll find there is nothing the enemy works harder to destroy than your trust in Jesus. He does it best in times of crisis. Why should a loving God let this happen to me?

As Jesus told the tale of the vineyard he was preparing his followers for the traumatic days they were about to face, days that could make them question everything Jesus had ever said to them. He didn't want their pain and confusion to destroy their trust. "In this world you will have trouble." But they would also have him if their mistrust didn't cause them to push him away.

Mistrust comes far more easily than any of us care to admit. I saw it one day in my then three-year-old son, Andy. It was early summer in the Sierra Nevada Mountains where my family had come to camp. As we prepared our evening meal we could hear the distant rumble of thunder move ever closer to our camp. A late-afternoon thunderstorm was building in around us.

We began our dinner to the sound of raindrops popping the blue tarp spread out above our table. Flashes of lightning photographed our little camp as the storm grew closer. The thunder grew louder, our children increasingly nervous. "Is it coming here?" Andy asked. The edges of his lips curled upward, expecting the answer he didn't want to hear.

"It's on its way," I said, hoping my flippant attitude would reassure him. Just to be safe I added, "But there's nothing to be afraid of." The scowl on his face told me I had not succeeded.

I kept my eye on Andy as he continued to eat half-heartedly. He listened to every thunder roll as the storm approached. Each time he would grimace until the rumbles finally dissipated into the forest around us.

FLASH! Our camp lit up as if a thousand flashbulbs had suddenly gone off.

CRACK! KA-BOOM! Instantly the thunder exploded. The concussion was so loud you could feel it. A lightning bolt had hit a rock on the hill behind us.

No one moved as we listened to the thunder chase down the nearby valleys. The rain fell harder now against the tarp. The eyes of our five-year-old daughter stood wide open, her mouth agape. I don't think she blinked for five minutes, but she looked more surprised than afraid, and I wasn't nearly so worried about her. Andy, however, slowly looked up from his plate, his eyes full of fear and his shoulders hunched up to his ears.

"What was that?"

"That noise?" I feigned surprise that he would even ask. I knew my next few words were critical. This was one of those brief but tenuous moments where the right words will save a flood of tears. I groped to find them. "It's just the storm. Lightning hit the hill behind us."

He thought about it for a minute. "Who did that?" His mouth tightened with anger. Andy is a lot like his dad; he finds any crisis easier to weather if he can find someone to blame it on—a most unfortunate inheritance.

But maybe this was my out. In our three short years with Andy we had taught him about God's love. Even if he didn't fully understand, he did know that God had created all things, that he loved us enough to send his own Son to die on the cross, and that he cares about the challenges we face.

"God did!" I smiled, hopeful that if he knew God was involved, his security in God's love would redefine his fear of the storm. God is good. He made the storm. Andy need not be afraid. Looking back, I don't know what possessed me to make such an assumption.

Immediately Andy's mind began to churn. We watched as he tried to bring these new facts together, like a computer trying to correlate conflicting data. After what must have been an entire 30 seconds, he looked up from under his forehead and announced between gritted teeth, "I don't want him to do it anymore."

Sara and I caved in with laughter, and that at least set him at ease. We at least avoided the crying spell that usually puts more focus on fear. But the price hadn't been cheap.

We could argue as to whether or not God had put that exact lightning bolt into the rock behind our camp, and whether my attempts to reassure my son were well-placed, but the upshot of the day was simple: This was the first time the simplicity of Andy's faith lost to the reality of his circumstances. Until now it was enough for him to accept that God loved him and could be trusted with his life. That had won us battles over swimming lessons and dark nights in his bedroom.

This time his fear was too great. Instead of viewing his circumstances through God's character, he judged God's character by his circumstances. Maybe God can't be trusted. Maybe his intentions are not all good. The unknown produced the same mistrust in him that it did in Adam and Eve in the Garden. He could only express his displeasure at God and the desire to control any future actions that might result in his discomfort.

That evening we watched our little boy begin a journey on which we've all embarked, and over which our faith must win. Certainly it is only part of growing up, but when our flesh begins to serve up cause for unbelief it's one of the worst parts. Those who define God's love by what happens to them in this age will for the most part be wrong. It is only an attempt to measure God's love by human wisdom.

"Remain in my love." How much more simply could Jesus have said it? No matter what the challenge; no matter how right our perspective may appear, invest your trust in him, today, and every day for the rest of your life. Then you'll know the depth of life-long friendship.

Invest your trust in him, today, and every day for the rest of your life. Then you'll know the depth of life-long friendship.

It was only lightning that day for our son, and he has long since moved past it. But what of his future and ours? Will our security in God's love win over misunderstood suffering, unanswered prayers, months of unemployment, or the abuse of friends? This is the essence of fire-tested faith. It endures even the events we cannot understand, and finds its resolve in knowing that God is wholly good and that he can be trusted with our lives. It is only out of this trust that we can discover that the mystery of God's grace and wisdom will always be enough to help us overcome in any situation.

At the end of his life, alone in a prison cell in Rome, realizing that the churches in Asia were quickly deserting the true gospel for cheap imitations, Paul declared with absolute certainty, "I have kept the faith."

Maybe that's all we're asked to do. Amidst the struggles and fears, the confusions and doubts, don't let go of faith no matter what. Jesus is the only thing solid enough to cling to in all the universe.

Everything else is just passing thunder.

13

LIFE-GIVING NOURISHMENT

*If you remain in me
and my words remain in you...*
JOHN 15:7

Tying vines is potentially the most painful of farm duties. Each cane remaining on a freshly pruned vine must be wrapped around the wire before the sap begins to flow. Often that put us out in the vineyard while frost still clung to the canes. Since we were paid for tying by how many vines we completed, speed was of the essence.

Every once in a while, however, in my haste I wouldn't get all the canes tightly secured. One of them would slip off the wire, pick up speed as it uncoiled itself, and smack me on my frozen cheek. I don't know if you've ever been slapped in the face on a subfreezing morning, but I can only commend it as an excellent form of torture.

For me, pain was almost always followed by anger, and often before rationality set in I would rip the cane out of the vine for its vile deed. Only then would the destruction I had caused sink home. Not wanting to be caught tying a vine with four canes when they're all supposed to have five, I would shove the base of the cane back into a cranny in the vine and tie it back on the wire. No one would be the wiser.

At least not until the sap flowed. And though it still might be stuck into the vine, we've already seen that if it is not attached to the vine, nothing will happen. Not one bud will swell, not one leaf will sprout.

The most significant contribution the vine makes to the branch can't even be seen by someone walking through the vineyard. It goes on deep beneath the scraggly bark. Through small capillary tubes, nutrients and water flow up through the roots, travel through the trunk, and spread out through every branch until they reach every leaf and maturing grape bunch. This life-giving sap makes the difference between a branch that is fruitful and one that is fit only for destruction.

The only time you get to see this flow of sap is early in the spring, before the vine fully shoots. Hanging on the end of each trimmed cane is often a small drop of sap. In the low-lined morning light these drops reflect like diamonds, a sure sign that spring is at hand and the sap is once again flowing in the vines.

That sap is what the vine gives to the branch to make it fruitful. Like the branches in the vine it is not enough that we are just near the presence of Jesus, we must be linked to him in a way that nourishes our lives. We are not transformed by just having read the Bible or having gone to church, but only to the extent that those things have allowed the life of Jesus to flow into ours.

Like the branches in the vine it is not enough that we are just near the presence of Jesus, we must be linked to him in a way that nourishes our lives.

How can we know if that is happening? Jesus gave his disciples one sure test. "If you remain in me *and my words remain in you*." The nourishment he gives us is in the words he speaks to us. If we are remaining in him, his words will fill our lives.

This is the first of four distinct qualities of our relationship with Jesus that he specifically highlights in the parable of the vineyard. Each one demonstrates not only what the vine provides to the branches, but also how the branches respond so as to remain in the vine. Here and in the next three chapters we'll take each of these in turn:

- Our friendship with Jesus is built on revelation, as he makes clear to us the ways of the Father.
- Our friendship with Jesus allows us to make requests of him with a reasonable certainty that he will give us what we ask.
- Our friendship with Jesus grows only as we obey him.
- Our friendship with Jesus calls for sacrifice; not only his for us, but ours on his behalf as well.

Let's begin with the first—our friendship is built on revelation. Your closest friends know the most about you, and you about them. Throughout the lesson of the vineyard this theme keeps popping up. At its beginning Jesus told the disciples that they were clean, or freshly pruned, by the words he'd spoken to them. At its end he told them that his words of revelation define the nature of their relationship. He didn't want them to be his servants, but his friends:

> *"I no longer call you servants, because a servant does not know his master's business. Instead, I have called you friends, for everything that I learned from my Father I have made known to you."*
>
> JOHN 15:15

Servants know only what they need to know to get their work done and are not invited in on the whole panorama of family life. Jesus, however, invites his followers to a far more intimate relationship. He wants us to know who he is and what he is like; and what he is doing in our lives so that we can share in it with him. Jesus does this in our lives ny revealing himself and his ways to us.

There are two important ways this revelation takes place in our lives. The first should be most obvious—Scripture itself. Those who desire to be linked to the vine will be students of Scripture. Here is God's full revelation, recorded so that at any moment we can pick it up and know who he is and what he is doing in our lives.

**Those who desire to be linked to the vine
will be students of Scripture.**

Like worship we discussed earlier, this is one of those places where Jesus has clearly invested his presence. He inhabits Scripture and every bit of it speaks of him. On the way to Emmaus the resurrected Lord began with Moses and all the prophets explaining to his unsuspecting companions "what was said in all the Scriptures concerning himself."

If we want God's fullness of joy and fruitfulness in all situations, it is important that we cultivate a regular feeding pattern from his Word. That will allow Jesus the opportunity to teach us his ways and by it transform our lives. Those who seek to follow Jesus will want to learn how to read it, study it, reflect on it and interpret it accurately.

Recently a friend of my co-pastor was going through a very difficult time. He had been laid off work with what appeared to be incredible underhandedness by his employer. Frustrated over a situation suddenly gone bad, and unsure of what else God would have in mind for his future income, he was desperately seeking direction.

"What have you been hearing in your Bible readings these days?" my co-pastor asked him.

"What?"

"Haven't you been having some time in the Word?"

"Well, to be honest, this work stuff has been so distracting I haven't gotten to it."

As my co-pastor related this conversation he shook his head in disbelief, "The time someone needs the Word the most, they give it up." We all need to have God's Word filling our lives. Even Jesus used the power of Scripture to turn back the temptations of Satan.

The "words" Jesus referred to that night with his disciples are not completely fulfilled by Scripture alone. The force of his encouragement goes beyond that to a believer's *ongoing perception of his words*. The second way Jesus wants to reveal his life to us is by speaking to each of us personally. He still speaks today, and learning to recognize his voice is a critical ingredient in our ability to enjoy the full glory of our friendship with him.

The second way Jesus wants to reveal his life to us is by speaking to each of us personally.

I realize I'm sailing into deep and dangerous waters here. The mere mention of God speaking to people today incites a host of responses. Some jump at the idea, ready to fulfill their most bizarre or selfish dreams while proclaiming that God told them to do so. Others reject it out of their own inexperience, mistakenly assuming that because they haven't learned to recognize God's voice, others can't either. Many see it as a threat to Scripture's authority, because some people claim revelations equal to the authority of Scripture, and usually superseding it when the two conflict.

These deceptions notwithstanding, our God is a God of revelation. He delights in making himself known to his people and leading them in his ways. He has a long history of doing exactly that, from his personal appearances to Enoch, Noah, Abraham, and others, to the revelation of his law and his counsel through his prophets.

Finally, God spoke again in the greatest revelation of all—his own Son, the exact representation of God himself. Did God's revealing nature end there? It did not.

Jesus himself told his disciples just after his tale of the vineyard that he had much more to tell them. But because they were unable to hear it he entrusted that revelation to the work of the Holy Spirit (John 16:12). Though the Spirit does not appear in our passage concerning the vineyard, he is the primary character in the context from which it springs. From John 14 through John 16 one of the major theme of Jesus' words center on the coming Comforter who would take Jesus' place in teaching, leading, and guiding his followers daily.

Jesus wanted his disciples to know that they wouldn't have to go on alone, trying to make do with the best applications of all he had said to them. When the Holy Spirit came on the day of Pentecost Peter announced that this was the fulfillment of God's promise to reveal himself to all who follow him. The result, demonstrated throughout the early church, was a people empowered by God's presence and sensitive to his voice.

This promise was extended to everyone the Father would call to himself from then on (Acts 2:39). His revelation continues even to the present. God's activity on our behalf didn't end with Scripture's completion.

Whenever God condemns idol worship, he expresses his incredulity that people would want to worship anything they could make themselves that cannot speak or act on their behalf. Isaiah taunted Israel with the sheer contradiction of building an idol out of the same piece of wood from which they had cut kindling to cook supper. Silent gods are false gods. People prefer them because they would rather follow their own idea of a god than serve the awesome, transcendent God of the ages.

To embrace God's revealing nature, however, doesn't devalue Scripture one bit. In fact it does just the opposite. The Scriptures are the *complete* revelation of all that God is and all that he comes to do in behalf of men. Anything the Spirit speaks today will only apply the truths of Scripture to the immediacy of our circumstances. But that continued disclosure is exactly what Jesus offered us.

Anything the Spirit speaks today will only apply the truths of Scripture to the immediacy of our circumstances.

Scripture is the only place where we can develop sensitivity to God's voice. These are God's words absolutely, and learning to hear him there will help us recognize his thoughts when he breathes them into our hearts.

Measuring our thoughts against Scripture is also the only objective test we have to distinguish the difference between our thoughts and God's. The apostle Paul warned us that our perception of God's voice in this life would not come with absolute clarity. He compared it to a poor reflection in a mirror (1 Corinthians 13:12). Though it is still a valuable vantage point we have to recognize that we will not see perfectly until we are transformed at his coming. Therefore we respect how easily colored our discernment might be by our own preferences and desires. If our perceptions of God's voice don't square with Scripture, whether in content or intent, they can be soundly rejected. For God will never act in a way that violates what he's already revealed about himself.

The friendship Jesus offered his followers hinges on intimate communication. Jesus wants you to know what the Father is doing in your life and in situations around you. He doesn't want you to grope around in uncertainty, and has offered you his ever-present voice.

But there are times when, despite our best efforts in prayer or study, we remain confused, unsure of the Father's will for us. We usually cycle through feelings of condemnation that he isn't being clear with us because we've done something wrong, to anger that he is holding back on us; to the mistaken conclusion that God doesn't speak today so we'll make do without it.

It's too bad that the very words Jesus spoke to comfort us in difficult moments are the ones that leave us most frustrated. I can't always tell you why at times it is more difficult to hear his voice. I do know he's promised to disclose to us what the Father is doing so that we don't have to guess what he's up to or resign ourselves to fatalism. That's a depth of communication I keep pressing toward because he's offered it.

Developing this discernment is a lifelong venture for a branch. I've no doubt God speaks to all of his followers daily; it's just that we don't always recognize his voice. It is easily drowned out by the clamor of circumstances, our fears, or our own desires.

But if we will continue to immerse ourselves in his Word and listen quietly for his voice we will learn to hear his voice with increasing clarity. Where is Jesus leading me today? What is he teaching me? What attitude or appetite is he dealing with, and how do I cooperate with him to see that work completed?

Remaining in those words is how we draw the nourishment of the vine. There is no greater treasure in our friendship with Jesus than this.

14

WHATEVER
I ASK?

*Ask whatever you wish, and
it will be given you.*
JOHN 15:7

In our understanding of the vineyard the contrasts between my father's vineyard and the Father's have been as significant as the similarities. Now we come to the most incredible contrast of all, for which there is not even a remote example in the vineyards of this earth.

In God's vineyard the branches themselves can make requests of the gardener that he promises to fulfill! What an awesome thought! I never heard a branch on any of the thousands of vines dotting my father's land ever make a request, much less get it answered.

The second quality of friendship Jesus pressed on his disciples was the open door to pursue our requests of him with a certainty that he will give us what we ask. It reveals yet another place where we go to remain in his presence—prayer. Not only does he want to speak to us, but he also invites us to speak to him, disclosing ourselves to him. Everyone who follows him needs a prayer closet, a time and place to regularly draw away to prayer. Why? Because the Almighty God who spoke worlds into existence invites you to ask whatever you wish from him *and* promises that he will give it.

The Almighty God who spoke worlds into existence invites you to ask whatever you wish from him *and* promises that he will give it.

Regretfully, however, instead of being awed by this promise, it is too often a source of great frustration. Such a promise is only credible if God actually backs it up, and most believers have a backlog of unanswered prayers that seems to make mockery of it. *Whatever* we ask we can have? Who is he trying to fool?

I read this passage to my children this morning as part of breakfast devotions. When I got done reading it, Andy, my ten-year-old son (who rarely makes comments about anything from the Bible), immediately responded, "That isn't true." His tone wasn't accusing or frustrated, just matter-of-fact.

"What do you mean?"

"What you just read: It doesn't really happen."

I was sure what he meant, but I asked him which part anyway so I could hear from his own lips what lurked in his young mind.

"It says whatever you wish for you can have. I have wished for a big-screen TV and I don't have one." Case closed.

"It doesn't say we can have what we wish for, but what we ask for. Have you ever asked for one?" Don't worry, I knew I was on thin ice here.

"Dad, can I have a big-screen TV?"

"It doesn't say to ask me." I asked Andy if he had ever prayed about this, and he honestly said he hadn't. Then we talked about whether we should ask God for something like that, and his response was, "It says `whatever you ask...'"

I'll grant you that the promise Jesus makes in this passage appears all-inclusive. At face value it suggests a 100-percent return on any request we make. Who, however, has an answered prayer list that reflects that standard of success? Anything less can become a source of frustration and disappointment.

How easy it is to overlook all the times God has answered our prayers when our latest request is seemingly on the back burner, if it made it to the kitchen at all. It is no wonder people eventually give up on prayer, either convinced that God doesn't really answer prayers today or at least won't for someone like them.

Our prayer theology is finally reduced to nothing more than throwing up a request and hoping for the best, like filling out a requisition form. Ship it upstairs and maybe if you're good enough, or if your request is pure enough, you might get what you ask for. But most times you don't, so don't expect much. After all, God knows what's best.

On the surface, such thinking sounds wonderfully biblical and wholly submitted to the Master's desires, but it flies in the face of the very certainty about our prayers that Jesus put forth to the branches in his vineyard. There is a place in him, he said, where we can ask for anything and *know* that we will get it.

Don't let the disappointments and imperfections of the past rob you of this hope and therefore short-circuit the process for getting there. Like almost every other promise in Scripture, it is not intended to frustrate you but designed to stimulate your growth until it is fulfilled.

Let us apply the same patience to growing in effective prayer that we do breaking free of the sins that entangle us. Both mandate a process that God invites us to embrace with hope. We would do far better growing in this process if we would shift our focus away from the frustration that accompanies unanswered prayers to being awed every time God *does* move in response to our prayers. That puts the focus in the right place and encourages our further growth.

Jesus' promise of answered prayer is not without precondition. We can have whatever we ask, *"if,"* as he already said, "you remain in me and my words remain in you." Jesus isn't hiding anything here. Our effectiveness in prayer flows out of the depth of intimacy we have established with the vine. If we're drawing our life from him, and allowing his words to have access to every corner of our lives, then (and only then) we can expect our prayers to be answered.

One of the things that most baffles me is when believers miss this connection between intimate relationship and answered prayer. Those who plow into their jobs or recreations with a fervor, leaving no time to cultivate the presence of Jesus, will be the first to complain when God doesn't meet their expectations. How can we fairly expect Jesus to respond to our requests if we are blatantly ignoring his?

I know such talk smacks of earning God's favor by our own sacrifice. Nothing could be further from the truth— not for our salvation nor for prayer. This is not a trade-off turning in Bible-reading credits for answered prayer. Something far deeper is at stake when we learn to remain in him and his words. By staying close enough to Jesus to know what he desires, we will find our desires being transformed to match his.

By staying close enough to Jesus to know what he desires, we will find our desires being transformed to match his.

In C.S. Lewis' fourth book of the Narnia series, *The*

Silver Chair, Prince Caspian arrives in heaven and expresses one of his desires to Aslan, the Christ-symbol. "Is that wrong?" he asked.

"You cannot want wrong things anymore, now that you have died, my son!" We can experience that same reality here as we die to our own desires. Jesus wants us to find a place in prayer where every request can be answered, because every request is a godly one.

It is impossible for us to remain in him and use prayer for our own gain or convenience. Not only do wrong prayers reinforce the wrong motives, answering them just isn't possible from God's perspective. How often do you think prayers by well-meaning believers motivated by personal desires would conflict with the prayers of others?

What if God only let it rain in the San Joaquin Valley when someone prayed for it? That would be fine if there were just one person to contend with, but when you add many people, who would he listen to? No matter when it rains in our part of the San Joaquin Valley, someone's crop is hurt by it. During our recent five-year drought we had what even our media termed a "Miracle March." Seven inches of rain fell in that month, almost two-thirds of our normal yearly total.

As elated as most people were with the rain, the media was still able to find farmers for whom the rain brought suffering. Fruit trees with tender blossoms were most at risk. Some trees the hail stripped, while others couldn't be pollinated normally because the bees were grounded in the inclement weather. Cotton farmers lamented that they couldn't get into the fields to plant.

Can you imagine God trying to respond to those varied requests? Even if he could get all the farmers to agree on rain at the same time, someone else would have planned a church picnic for the same day, and a whole flock of believers would pray against it. Regardless of what happened, some people would be overjoyed that their prayers were answered because they got what they wanted, while those who didn't would wonder why God doesn't love them. If we're going to get serious about answered prayer we're going to have to stop trying to use God for our own trivial convenience. Jesus only interfered with the weather one time and it wasn't to save a church picnic. The promise of John 15 was not intended to be a tool for our own comfort.

Neither can it be taken apart from Jesus' other instructions about prayer. Remember when James and John asked for fire to come down from heaven to consume the Samaritans for not welcoming Jesus? Far from answering their request, Jesus rebuked the spirit from which it came. And Jesus could not grant Peter's desire to derail him from going to the cross without circumventing a higher plan of God.

Scripture gives many other reasons why our prayers go unanswered, and it is well for us to search them out. They are not intended to rob us of the certainty of God answering our prayers. Rather they are to show us why he sometimes doesn't, so that we can dispense with those kinds of prayers.

When Jesus promised his disciples around that grapevine that he wanted to answer whatever request they would make of him, his purpose was not centered in them at all, but in God and his mission: "This is to my Father's glory, that you bear much fruit, showing yourselves to be my disciples" (John 15:8). God moving in response to our prayers accomplishes three things:

First, it brings glory to the Father. When God's power moves in our lives beyond our own abilities or plans, it testifies to his presence. People's attentions are drawn to the Father and not to our skills. God is glorified by answering the godly requests of his people.

Second, God's answers are a key ingredient to our bearing fruit. Developing an intimacy of relationship with the vine does demand confidence that we can draw from him what we need. Without that active involvement we won't be able to produce anything fruitful in his kingdom, any more than a branch can produce fruit if it doesn't receive nourishment consistently from the vine. This also hints at the direction of our prayers. Instead of praying for God to save us out of difficult circumstances we will instead pray for that which will bring the greatest glory to God, which as we said earlier will produce in us the fruits of his Spirit.

Instead of praying for God to save us out of difficult circumstances we will instead pray for that which will bring the greatest glory to God.

Finally, God's answers demonstrate an intimacy of friendship that testifies to God's reality in our lives and gives others hope of finding the same relationship as well. How often the disciples were enamored by Jesus' prayers! They could see how the Father immediately responded to his requests for a storm to be stilled, blind eyes healed, and sinful people forgiven. "Teach us to pray" was not an attempt to learn a spiritual discipline, but to find out how to effectively connect with the Father. They wanted that same relationship, and so will others as they see him at work in us.

For all these reasons God wants to respond to our prayers with complete fulfillment, even more than we want him to. When he doesn't, this should signal us that perhaps our request was wrong or that some wrong motives have twisted their way into our prayer. If we don't go on to probe why not, we'll never become more effective in prayer and merely consign ourselves to sending requests and settling for whatever we're fortunate enough to get.

In the same way we should never get smug about the prayers he does answer, as if we in our goodness somehow deserve them. Nothing we've covered in this chapter is intended to communicate that answered prayers are to be worn as merit badges. Though unanswered prayer is a good indicator of how much more deeply we can grow in the vine, answered prayers are not something to boast in. Sometimes God moves in spite of us as much as because of us, and any boasting runs counter to the fruit he wants to produce in us.

God wants to teach us through our praying how to zero in on his will, and how to bring it into reality through prayer. His goal is unchanged: He wants to give us *whatever* we ask. If we'll remain in him he will teach us. It's one of the lessons he wants all of his branches to learn well.

15

GOING
MY WAY?

If you obey my commands, you will
remain in my love.... You are my friends
if you do what I command.
JOHN 15:10,14

A certain farmer had two sons. One morning he went to the first and told him he needed him to work in the vineyard that day. "I will not!" the son answered.

How I can relate to that! Every time my dad wanted me in the vineyard, I didn't want to go. My three brothers and I spent Christmas vacations pruning vines, Easter breaks hoeing weeds, and the last weeks before school picking grapes. Saturdays brought further opportunities to tie vines, pick up discarded branches, or box raisins. I got sick of working in the vineyard. I guess we all did, since none of us ended up back on the farm.

So I relate well to this son's desire not to work in the vineyard, although I'm not so sure I would have answered my father as abruptly as he did. My father was very fond of that "when-I-say-jump-you-only-ask-how-high" philosophy of parenting. I rarely rebelled so openly, though it did cross my mind.

Afterward, however, the son repented of his attitude and left whatever else he was doing to begin work in the vineyard (Matthew 21:28-32). What might have triggered his change of heart we're not told. Jesus doesn't say the father argued with him or punished him for his insolence. He just went on to the second son and made the same request.

"I will, sir!" was the second son's response. Our hearts are warmed by his quick choice of obedience, and by the words of respect with which he answers his father. This is the kind of son anyone would want—ready for obedience at a moment's notice.

Well, not quite. Ready to *talk* obedience at any moment was closer to the truth. Again we're not told why, but this son never made it to the vineyard. Perhaps he had no intent to obey, only dismissing his father by telling him what he wanted to hear. The vineyard could have been large enough that his father would not have known anyway. Or maybe he wanted to obey, but in the going was distracted by a better offer—by a friend to go swimming at the creek, perhaps.

Having told this simple story, Jesus asked an even simpler question, which no one would have hesitated to answer correctly. "Which of the two did what his father wanted?"

"The first," they answered.

This was one of my favorite parables growing up because it had great value in keeping my parents off-balance. I'm pretty sure Jesus didn't teach this parable for the reason I used it, but when my parents told me to work for them, I would often respond like the first brother: "I will not." I could see their jaws set and their eyes squint, but before they could say anything I was off to the task they had asked of me. What could they say? It drove them nuts. No one likes to be told no, but I would refer them to this parable and they would only shake their heads in frustration.

Even though my application was selfishly motivated, this parable intends to make exactly that point. What matters in the kingdom of God is obedience—not the intent to obey, or the promise to, but the actual act, even if it comes after initial resistance. He would prefer both, of course, the expression of obedience and the act, but the parable makes clear the act is the most important.

This parable was not told to Jesus' disciples, but to the chief priests and elders who had interrupted him in their latest attempt to trap him into offending the adoring crowds around him. They were the ones who answered his question so easily and the ones to suffer the full force of the parable's conclusion. "I tell you the truth, the tax collectors and the prostitutes are entering the kingdom of God ahead of you."

These leaders gave the appearance of pursuing God, but somehow never got to the task. While their mouths said "I will," their lives said "Sorry, not now." Sinners, on the other hand, whose lives started out with a great big no, ended up in the Father's vineyard.

It is always easier to follow God with our mouths than with our lives, and the danger doesn't diminish with our longevity on the vine. Religious forms and traditions are easier to follow than simply doing the things God asks of us each day.

It is always easier to follow God with our mouths than with our lives, and the danger doesn't diminish with our longevity on the vine.

Jesus didn't want his disciples to meet a similar end. The third quality of friendship that Jesus highlighted in his parable of the vineyard is incredibly special. It is true in no other friendship they would ever have. "If you obey my commands, you will remain in my love, just as

I have obeyed my Father's commands and remain in his love."

Our participation in the vineyard is not a merging of two branches. Quite the contrary, our lives are planted onto the one, true vine. Even though that relationship is defined by the tenderness of intimate friendship, we must never forget that this is not a friendship between equals. The branch draws from the vine, not the other way around.

We must never forget that this is not a friendship between equals. The branch draws from the vine, not the other way around.

Jesus hangs the continued development of our friendship with him on our obedience *to* him. In case they missed it the first time, he says it again a bit differently four sentences later: "You are my friends if you do what I command."

Who else could ever make such a statement? Try it with your spouse or one of your friends, and see where it gets you. When you think the mood is just right lean over to them and say, "I'll always be your friend if you do everything I want you to do."

Sounds absurd, doesn't it? We understand that friendships grow through give-and-take, each person offering something to it and drawing value from it. When disagreements emerge we seek to incorporate the best insights of both in finding a solution that will best address all concerns.

Apply those same ideas to your relationship with Jesus, however, and you will find yourself drying up on the vine. There is only one way to go in this vineyard and it is his. Why is it different with Jesus? Because he has all wisdom and power. His judgments are not clouded with favoritism or selfish pursuits. He knows what is best for us, and for the development of our friendship with him.

Even in our passionate campaigns to get God to understand our concerns and insights, we can't lose sight of who he is. We don't ever have to battle him, but instead cultivate a heart of surrender and obedience. Nothing will affect the growth of your life with him more than this simple heart of submission.

Our friendship with him is marvelously one-sided, but that certainly doesn't mean it has to be any less intimate. He tenderly wants to share his presence with us and disclose to us all that the Father is doing around us. But this is not a place we come to *talk about* the things of God but *to give ourselves to them*. What he asks in return is that we not just hear his words but obey them.

Note the priority here. Obedience is one of the last things the branch is asked for, not the first. Many people try to cultivate their friendship with God by being obedient to some expectation they think God holds for them. They put off their pursuit of the Lord until they start going to church, give up smoking, or in some other way become a "better" person.

Obedience does not earn our acceptance, it flows out of it. Only as we have accepted Jesus' offer of friendship and been cleansed and nourished by the power of his words, do we have any understanding of what obedience means for us or any capacity to follow through with it. Remember, without him we can do nothing, absolutely nothing!

**Obedience does not earn our acceptance,
it flows out of it.... Remember,
without him we can do nothing,
absolutely nothing!**

Out of friendship and learning to clearly hear him we begin to understand what obedience means. Many people mistake obedience for perfection. It is not. Our struggle against the flesh is a lifelong war and more than any of us would like we'll fall prey to its appetites and deceptions. Jesus knows full well the weaknesses of our flesh, and the obedience he invites us to is not living up to a list of rules or expectations, but direction as timely as the circumstances of each day.

Jesus demonstrated this by how he treated Peter even before Peter was going to deny him. Just a few hours after Jesus challenged them to obedience Peter was headed to a battle with his flesh that he would lose. Though Jesus clearly did not want Peter to fail, he knew how weak he was and how easy it would be for him to succumb to his fears. It's interesting that Jesus didn't tell him not to deny him, nor did he encourage him to stay home out of harm's way. Instead he has already prayed for Peter that *after* his failure he would return again to strengthen the other disciples. Jesus knew that was all the obedience Peter could live up to that day and required nothing more.

Obedience, Jesus said, was the secret to remaining in his love. It had been no different between Jesus and his father: "Just as I have obeyed my Father's commands and remain in his love." Jesus had already set the example for the disciples. He had done everything the Father had asked him to do.

In the next few hours he would do it yet again. From this garden he would be thrust into the mockery, torture, and death that would procure our salvation. His strength through it came only as he surrendered to God, "Not as I will, but as you will." If Jesus wanted to remain in the Father's love he had to obey him in the midst of those dark hours.

What if Jesus had called a legion of angels to rescue him? Would God have loved him less? Of course not. But in his disobedience he would have removed himself from the care and protection of the Father's love and would have thwarted his plan of salvation. That's where many misunderstand the nature of God's love.

Yes, it is unconditional. He will love us no matter what, but Jesus isn't talking here about how much he loves us, but whether or not we'll receive that love and share in its power. I've sat with parents anguished by the rebellion of their own children. Though the parents still love them deeply, unless these children turn away from trouble and return to that love, they will not share in it.

It's a lesson I teach every couple who comes to my office wanting to get married. As much as I teach them the necessity of loving their partner without demanding that they meet certain expectations, I teach them that the quality of their marriage will hinge on obedience to the vows they will take. The depth of their friendship will depend upon how well they learn to cherish each other, care for each other, and endure the troubles of this age with each other *every* day.

The day we repented and were grafted into his vine our commitment was to forsake our own way and go his. Only by doing that will we continue to grow; and we will only be able to obey him to the degree that we walk in friendship with him.

It's what the branch does to stay linked to the vine. Our love for him will flow over into the desire to walk in his will. That combination will ensure that we will be fruitful in every circumstance and every day discover greater depths of intimacy with him.

16

DIE
TO IT!

Greater love has no one than this, that he lay down his life for his friends.
JOHN 15:13

Caring for a vineyard is hard work.

Not a season goes by that there isn't something the farmer has to do if he is going to have a fruitful vineyard. Many plants will at least bear some fruit in the wild, but not the grapevine. It cannot even support its own branches. They must be painstakingly tied on a wire to keep the fruit and canes off of the ground. If it is not pruned every year, all the energy of the vine will be spent producing leaves and none producing fruit. So month after month the farmer is in the vineyard.

He prunes.

He ties.

He waters.

He shovels.

He sprays.

He picks.

None of these tasks requires a great deal of talent or offers any deep sense of accomplishment. They are menial, dirty tasks often demanding to be done even in the harshest conditions—the blazing heat of summer or the biting cold of winter.

Some people even consider the work demeaning, similar to how the disciples felt about a different task a few hours before their trip to the vineyard. They had come to the upper room with feet soiled from dusty lanes of the city. Since their room was rented there was no designated host to make sure the guests' feet were washed.

How awkward those first moments in the room must have been! Lots of dirty feet and no one willing to wash them. They must have thought about it, certain that someone else was supposed to do it. Let Judas, he paid for the room. What about Bartholomew? He was the last one chosen, wasn't he? They ultimately decided to skip it altogether and pretend their feet weren't dirty, because dinner was already being served and no one had volunteered to wash the others' feet.

That is until Jesus tied a towel around his waist. Though some obviously didn't want *him* to do it, no one else offered. So he washed their feet. Some have suggested that Jesus did so to teach them humility. John disagreed. He said Jesus washed their feet expressly to show them "the full extent of his love" (John 13:1). This was not a show. It was a photograph of love in its most complete form. Jesus cared about them enough to do the most menial task for them.

"Greater love has no one than this, that he lay down his life for his friends." The fourth and final quality of friendship that Jesus delineates in his tale of the vine is that our friendship with him calls for sacrifice. Friends give up their lives for each other.

Jesus was that kind of friend. Though he would prove it again in a few hours on a brutal cross, he'd already shown them the extent of his love when he didn't consider it beneath his dignity to wash dirty feet. He loved them, even the one who would betray him.

When we consider his call to absolute obedience, remember who it is that asks it of us. This is one who will not use our obedience for his own gain. We are compelled to trust someone like that, no matter what adversity we face. The apostle Paul reflected on it time and again when he was tempted in the midst of crisis to believe Jesus didn't care for him. If Jesus would go to such lengths to save me when I was a sinner, would he really deny me anything I need to find my way into His life now that I'm seeking to follow him? (compare Romans 8:32).

But there is a larger lesson here. The love Jesus demonstrated is the love he asked from the disciples. I want you to lay down your lives for me as well. How? By dying on a cross?

No, he had something else in mind. Even though most if not all of the disciples in that circle would eventually die for him, their death was not the sacrifice he sought. "Love each other as I have loved you." He instead called them to lay down their lives for him by laying it down for each other. Perhaps this is the harder of the two. Sometimes it is easier to die for someone than to live alongside them.

Except for the call to remain in him, this is the only other lesson of the vineyard that Jesus repeats. He follows his call to obedience by his one command: Love one another. This is the obedience upon which all other obediences hang.

**Love one another.
This is the obedience upon which all
other obediences hang.**

It is a familiar call to anyone who has been a Christian for very long, but don't let that distract from the power of his simple statement. This was not an abstract call to love all of God's people. There were only 12 people in that vineyard on the evening Jesus told his tale. I wonder if Jesus even gestured around the circle as he spoke the words. For the love he asked of them couldn't be hidden in generalities. These men knew each other, weaknesses and all. Surely he doesn't mean the power-grabbing Zebedee boys. Or Peter, the man who would be our leader except that he can't get his foot out of his mouth long enough to be of much use. Certainly he doesn't mean Thomas whose incessant questioning drives us all nuts.

Here is where love is tested, and here is where the lesson of the vineyard reaches its conclusion. For we have arrived back at the beginning. The fruit that God is coaxing out of each of us is his love. This is the testimony the world cannot refuse.

This is the fruit of our remaining in him and the command that fulfills all others:

> You, my brothers, were called to be free. But do not use your freedom to indulge the sinful nature; rather, serve one another in love. The entire law is summed up in a single command: "Love your neighbor as yourself." If you keep on biting and devouring each other, watch out or you will be destroyed by each other.
>
> GALATIANS 5:13,14

Nothing will destroy our flesh faster than learning to love the people around us through the most menial forms of service. The world teaches us to be preoccupied with our own needs and ambitions. Jesus, however, offered us the opportunity to lay down our lives for him by being a blessing to others. Learning to love that way is part of God's plan to reverse the world's agenda. No longer preoccupied with our own desires, we become part of God's work to touch others.

Recently our church sponsored a youth outreach to three unreached villages in central Mexico. Thirty-two people went down over Easter break, a prime opportunity to learn the depths of love. Dan, one of the leaders of the outreach, came back with an amazing story that became a powerful lesson for me.

Everything does not always run smoothly on such trips, and it's easy for people to get on your nerves. Virtually every time Dan got frustrated by someone else, God saw to it that a missionary we worked with in that area was nearby. Seeing Dan's frustration begin to build, he would quietly sneak behind Dan and whisper in his ear, "Dan, die to it!" That was all, nothing more. But a gentle smile would sneak past Dan's lips as he would give in to the vital message it held.

Not all wars are meant to be fought, not all preferences have to be championed, not all hurts need to be ironed out. Some things we can just die to, giving up what's in it for us and going on, washing the feet of others in a practical way. Dan's testimony of that lesson was like a splash of cool water on a hot face. What freedom! It reminded me about so many things I face in the fellowship here at home. I don't have to vent every frustration. Sometimes I can just die to it, trusting God to work his will without me pushing for my own way.

Not all wars are meant to be fought, not all preferences have to be championed, not all hurts need to be ironed out. Some things we can just die to.

Don't get me wrong; honesty and justice are valuable virtues for a body of believers growing in unity, but so also is the freedom to die to our wants.

What a testimony to others when believers love with such grace and deference to one another! What results is the deep fulfillment we spoke of earlier, joy as we've never known it because it rests in things far more eternal than our latest purchase or career achievement. We do not touch eternity any closer in this age than by sharing God's love for people.

Throughout the last few chapters I've emphasized that we remain in Jesus by being where he is. We've talked already about his presence in worship, prayer, and Scripture, and about his voice and our obedience. Now Jesus' command to love one another brings us to the last two places where we regularly confront the presence of Jesus: the community of believers, and people in need.

Jesus' command to love one another brings us to the last two places where we regularly confront the presence of Jesus: the community of believers, and people in need.

"For where two or three come together in my name, there am I with them" (Matthew 18:20). Jesus is present where believers come together to share his life. I'm talking way beyond church membership or attendance. Sitting in a large gathering watching all the action happen onstage doesn't even begin to approach the power of Jesus' call here.

Body life in the New Testament was not primarily centered in meetings, but relationships. Though I find great joy in gathering with large groups for worship and hearing the Word taught, it alone is not the community God desires. The early believers lived out their faith through intimate and mutually supportive contact with other believers.

The house church movement of this century is far closer to the biblical example, though certainly not the only model. You will find it helpful to a growing walk of intimacy if you have a circle of believers whose lives you can touch two or three times a week and with whom you can share encouragement, insight and opportunities to love each other.

As branches on the vine, our lives are linked together. This is an interesting vineyard Jesus talked about. It is a one-vine vineyard. Every branch grows from the same vine, Jesus.

On a grapevine, no branch lives independent of the others. When one is besieged, they all are. When one is in need, the others can help make up the difference. I've seen entire branches stripped of their leaves by voracious insects. Not a leaf left on the branch, and without leaves grapes won't sweeten. But these still did. Why? Because the sugar produced by the other branches on that vine found its way to the grapes on the denuded branch.

Anyone who tries to go it alone does so at his own peril. It's like trying to be a one-person softball team. No matter how good you are, there's no way you can win a ball game by yourself. How can you cover the whole field on defense? Who are you going to throw to? And when you're at bat you have to hit a home run every time or you're out, and who's capable of that?

Neither can we win alone in the kingdom of God, though I see many people try it. They'll come to church on Sunday and then to my office on Tuesday wanting help with some struggle. I tell them that to overcome, part of what they'll need to do is get involved in the lives of other believers. It's amazing. Those who do, get healed. Those who think they can make it on their own never overcome and never seem to figure out why.

Supportive, intimate friendships, the opportunities to serve, the added wisdom and strength, the lessons of forgiveness, and a place to be held accountable all grow out of our relationships with other believers and are all helpful in our growth in him. But let's not forget his command. It wasn't to get love from others, but to love others. Staying focused there will fulfill his command.

The last place Jesus clearly said he invested his presence is in ministry to the needy. "Whatever you did for one of the least of these brothers of mine, you did for me" (Matthew 25:40). He affirms his presence in the needs of his creation and tells us that our response to people in need, not just believers, is a response to him. We have been blessed by God to be a blessing to others.

Everyone who grows in friendship with Jesus will find regular opportunities to serve others in the daily course of their lives and can seek out opportunities to go into another person's world and serve. You don't have to go out of the country for these opportunities. Serving in a soup kitchen or tutoring an underprivileged child at your neighborhood school can be every bit as powerful as going on outreach in Asia. In my own city, Asia has already come to us in the form of refugees from Laos.

True Christlike love is foreign to our flesh and in the beginning it will be difficult learning to lay our lives down. But learning to live in love's freedom is one of the great pleasures of being a branch in this vineyard. It is always deeply fulfilling and full of surprises. We'll find ourselves doing and saying things to others that will astound us. "That's not me" and "I've never felt like that before" will become common refrains of wonder.

That's fruitfulness, and it will only arise as we lay our lives down for others, regardless of the resistance of our flesh.

"Die to it!" is the battle cry of a fruitful branch.

17

A WIDER VIEW: WORKERS IN THE VINEYARD

*Listen to another parable: There was a landowner
who planted a vineyard. He put a wall around it,
dug a winepress in it and built a watchtower.
Then he rented the vineyard to some farmers
and went away on a journey.*
MATTHEW 21:33

It was a conspiracy, plain and simple.

The workers huddled together against the wall at the vineyard's edge. For some time they had been watching a lonely figure making his way up the road to the vineyard, the dust of his feet billowing behind him in the still morning air. He was close enough now for all to recognize him. It was who they thought it was—the owner's son. For weeks they had been badgered by the master's servants coming to collect the fruit of the vineyard.

But they had already decided to keep the fruit for themselves, no matter the cost. Their final plan took shape quickly. "This is the heir. Come, let's kill him and take his inheritance."

As we end our study of Jesus' tale of the vine, let's take a wider look around the vineyard. To this moment we have primarily focused on Jesus' words in John 15 that picture us as branches drawing life from the vine.

But there is another analogy that Jesus used on numerous occasions regarding his vineyard. Not only can we be pictured as branches, but in his unique vineyard we are also workers. We've already seen this reflected in the parable of the workers who were hired throughout the day, and two brothers who were told to work in the vineyard. We'll examine one other tale that allows us a wider view of the vineyard and a final application of Jesus' words.

The image of the branches focused on our personal journey of faith. The analogy of us as workers highlights our involvement with the Father as he touches other believers around us in their journeys of faith. Jesus taught his followers that there were things they could do that would help promote his work in others, and as importantly he showed them ways they could overstep the limits of ministry to the detriment of others' faith.

Understanding this aspect of the vineyard takes us beyond our own personal discipleship, to understand the value of personal ministry as we live out his command to, "Love one another."

Interestingly enough, the parable of the workers in the vineyard comes directly on the heels of the short parable we examined two chapters ago about the two brothers who were asked by their father to go out and work in his field. From that story, Jesus launches into this one with the same priests and elders who worked so hard to thwart his ministry. Instead of exercising their role as leaders to help people into the life of God, they were doing all they could to make sure others were kept out. Jesus' story cuts to the heart of their motives, and in so doing serves as timely warning to any who labor in God's vineyard.

Let's go back to the beginning of Jesus' parable. The landowner planted a vineyard and dressed it with a wall to protect it, a watchtower to keep it safe, and a winepress to process its fruit. This was a first-class vineyard.

Then he rented out his vineyard to laborers. Leaving it to their care, he went on a journey. Harvest time came and went. The landlord sent his servants to collect the fruit. But these were not only greedy but vicious men. Instead of meeting their obligation they mistreated the landlord's servants. Some they beat, some they killed, and some they stoned.

Their final treason to slaughter the landlord's son was not formed overnight. For a long time the landowner sought their attention and could not get it. The same is true of us. Rejecting God's words is almost always the end of a long process of refusing God's gentle requests. The first time is always the hardest; then it gets easier and easier even as God makes more impressive overtures. We can even come to the point, like the workers in this parable, where we turn on Jesus himself.

Israel's long history of abusing God's messengers should be a clear warning for us. A similar phenomena exists in the history of the church. No one resists the fresh working of God in any age of the church quite like the church itself as it grows sluggish and institutionalized following previous times of renewal.

This should give us pause. Are we today listening to the voices we want to hear, or are we hearing those that God is sending today to call us to change? Have our institutions grown rigid? God always holds people in leadership accountable as to whether they make it easy for people to respond to God or difficult by their cumbersome rules and personal refusal to submit to the life of Jesus as he intended.

The landlord sent his son as the last resort. "They will respect my son."

But they did not. They had already decided to usurp the landlord's place in the vineyard and assume control by treason. They wanted all the fruit for themselves. Instead of serving God in his vineyard, they wanted the vineyard to serve them. So when they saw his son coming unprotected they knew how to secure final ownership of the land they craved. They threw the landlord's son out of the vineyard and killed him, thinking that now all would belong to them.

Here Jesus stops the parable and asks a question: "When the owner of the vineyard comes, what will he do to those tenants?" He waits for their answer. "He will bring those wretches to a wretched end and he will rent the vineyard to other tenants who will give him his share of the crop at harvest time" (Matthew 21:33-44).

Matthew thought it important enough to note that the chief priests and Pharisees knew that Jesus was talking about them. Most of the time they didn't understand his parables at all. He was accusing them of using God's work for their own gain, even to the point of committing murder to steal his vineyard.

Though this parable was especially directed at the leadership of Jesus' day, its application extends to all of us. For we are all called to minister Jesus' life to other believers around us. Paul minces no words about that: "In Christ we who are many form one body, and each member belongs to all the others" (Romans 12:5). I belong to other believers, and they to me. We do not have the luxury of being preoccupied with our own growth alone, for we are also his laborers to help others.

Though many of us will think first of "ministry" tasks we can carry out to help others, the primary biblical application of ministry grows out of personal friendships with other believers around us. Though these friendships can be grounded in a local fellowship as we've seen, it is by no means limited to it. We are to seek out fellowship and service to other believers regardless of whether they gather behind the same four walls we do on Sunday morning.

This parable reminds us that all that we discussed in

the previous chapters of God's work to make us fruitful and fulfilled in his kingdom he is also doing in others around us. We can share in that process if we keep in mind who owns the vineyard.

Jesus warned the Pharisees that at some point they shifted from just being workers in the Father's vineyard, to wanting something more—ownership of his work for themselves. They would benefit from its fruit instead of giving it back to God.

As branches we can never forget in whose vineyard we are growing; as workers that becomes even more critical. No matter how God chooses to use us, we cannot ever allow ourselves to think that his work in others is meant for our gain or pleasure. We can only serve well as we remember that all the fruit belongs to God.

If history is any teacher at all, we know how easy it is for us to lose sight of how *we can bless the vineyard* and to

---

As branches we can never forget in whose vineyard we are growing; as workers that becomes even more critical.

---

think instead of how *the vineyard can bless us*. The prophets in the Old Testament chided Israel's shepherds who misused the sheep for their own gain. Instead of risking their lives to keep the sheep happy, they butchered the sheep to fill their own bellies. In this same mixed metaphor Jeremiah showed us how we can abuse God's vineyard, "Many shepherds will ruin my vineyard and trample down my field… the whole land will be laid waste because there is no one who cares" (12:10-11).

This is God's vineyard. Everything we do in it must flow from *his* desires, and every produce of it belongs to him. He must receive what is due him, freely given from our hand. If not, the vineyard will waste away and he will have to remove us.

Jesus concludes his parable by identifying himself as the rejected cornerstone. Those who do not accept him will have the vineyard taken away from them and "given to a people who will produce its fruit" (Matthew 21:43).

I told you fruitfulness was God's passion, as much in our service to others as it is in our personal lives. As we've seen throughout the vineyard, that fruit is only produced where Jesus remains the central focus. That's as true for workers as it is for branches. He is the line of demarcation in all things spiritual. Are we following his voice and his desires, or are we only trying to do things for him for our own gain or blessing?

So we end where we began—the centrality of Jesus and his work on the cross. Whether as branches or as workers, we are free to trust him in every detail of our lives.

As branches we have no life in ourselves and no need to possess anything. Everything belongs to the Father and his Son and so it must remain so all our days. You'll be tempted to find life in other things—to want to grab on to some blessing of his and make an idol out of it. Just keep in mind the moral of the story is still the same: apart from him we can do nothing.

As workers, every fruit belongs to him. Whatever service we render is to build his kingdom not our own; whatever love we share with others is for his gain. Since we have all things from him, we never have to want for anything again.

Understand that, and you've grasped the mystery of Jesus' tale of the vine and you will know joy in abundance and fruitfulness beyond your wildest dreams.

The adventure continues...

Seasons
In the Vine

In this sequel to the *Tales of the Vine*, author Wayne Jacobsen goes back to the well of Scripture and his own experiences growing up on a vineyard to show how the changing seasons in the vineyard are an essential ingredient to its fruitfulness. The same is true in our journey of faith. Times of great promise are usually followed by hardship and challenge. Seasons of great fruitfulness are often followed by periods of dormancy and pruning where God re-stages us for another cycle of fruitfulness. If you've ever wondered why the circumstances around your life fluctuate so greatly and what God is doing in them to fulfill the deepest cries of your heart, you'll want to read *Seasons of the Vine*.

Available after May of 1996

Other Books by Wayne Jacobsen

The Naked Church

Clothed in expensive architecture, elaborate programs and impressive statistics, the modern church has all too often traded the presence of God for the nakedness of religious form. Wayne examines how we lost touch with the active presence of God as the focus of church life and offers a blueprint for how the reader can rediscover the power of spiritual intimacy. (Formerly titled *A Passion for God's Presence*)

Pathways of Grace

A seventeen-week workbook of daily Bible readings and weekly small-group discussions, to help believers develop their friendship with the Father and pass on their life in him to others.

• Seminars •

Wayne also travels the world helping people discover the simplicity and joy of a vital relationship with the Father through Jesus. He shares in church, retreat and classroom settings on such topics as:

- Intimacy with God
- The power of the cross
- The centrality of Jesus in body life
- The joy of Christian community
- Leadership training
- The wonder of a God-centered marriage

If you would like information regarding this ministry, or want to receive his newsletter, please contact BodyLife Resources:

(209) 635-8565
Fax: (209) 735-9288
On the internet: wjacobsen@aol.com

Also, as the director of BridgeBuilders, Wayne makes his time available to resolve tensions between public school educators and religious parents. By building a genuine, religious-neutral environment where the values of religious families are not undermined in the public forum, he is helping various groups find constructive ways to work together for benefit of all students.